MICROSERVICES

NOVICE TO NINJA

BUILD, DESIGN AND DEPLOY
DISTRIBUTED SERVICES

4 BOOKS IN 1

BOOK 1
MICROSERVICES 101: A BEGINNER'S GUIDE TO UNDERSTANDING
DISTRIBUTED SYSTEMS

BOOK 2
ARCHITECTING MICROSERVICES: STRATEGIES FOR DESIGNING
SCALABLE AND RESILIENT SYSTEMS

BOOK 3
MASTERING MICROSERVICES: ADVANCED TECHNIQUES FOR
OPTIMIZING PERFORMANCE AND SECURITY

BOOK 4
MICROSERVICES MASTERY: EXPERT INSIGHTS INTO DEPLOYMENT,
MONITORING, AND MAINTENANCE

ROB BOTWRIGHT

Published by Rob Botwright
Library of Congress Cataloging-in-Publication Data
ISBN 978-1-83938-701-2
Cover design by Rizzo

Disclaimer

The contents of this book are based on extensive research and the best available historical sources. However, the author and publisher make no claims, promises, or guarantees about the accuracy, completeness, or adequacy of the information contained herein. The information in this book is provided on an "as is" basis, and the author and publisher disclaim any and all liability for any errors, omissions, or inaccuracies in the information or for any actions taken in reliance on such information. The opinions and views expressed in this book are those of the author and do not necessarily reflect the official policy or position of any organization or individual mentioned in this book. Any reference to specific people, places, or events is intended only to provide historical context and is not intended to defame or malign any group, individual, or entity. The information in this book is intended for educational and entertainment purposes only. It is not intended to be a substitute for professional advice or judgment. Readers are encouraged to conduct their own research and to seek professional advice where appropriate. Every effort has been made to obtain necessary permissions and acknowledgments for all images and other copyrighted material used in this book. Any errors or omissions in this regard are unintentional, and the author and publisher will correct them in future editions.

BOOK 1 - MICROSERVICES 101: A BEGINNER'S GUIDE TO UNDERSTANDING DISTRIBUTED SYSTEMS

BOOK 2 - ARCHITECTING MICROSERVICES: STRATEGIES FOR DESIGNING SCALABLE AND RESILIENT SYSTEMS

BOOK 3 - MASTERING MICROSERVICES: ADVANCED TECHNIQUES FOR OPTIMIZING PERFORMANCE AND SECURITY

BOOK 4 - MICROSERVICES MASTERY: EXPERT INSIGHTS INTO DEPLOYMENT, MONITORING, AND MAINTENANCE

Introduction

Welcome to "Microservices: Novice to Ninja - Build, Design, and Deploy Distributed Services," a comprehensive book bundle that will take you on a journey from beginner to expert in the world of microservices architecture. In this bundle, we have carefully curated four essential volumes that cover everything you need to know about building, designing, and deploying microservices at scale.

BOOK 1 - MICROSERVICES 101: A BEGINNER'S GUIDE TO UNDERSTANDING DISTRIBUTED SYSTEMS: In this introductory volume, we lay the foundation for understanding distributed systems and microservices architecture. From the basic principles of decoupling and scalability to the challenges of fault tolerance and resilience, this book will provide you with a solid understanding of the core concepts that underpin microservices.

BOOK 2 - ARCHITECTING MICROSERVICES: STRATEGIES FOR DESIGNING SCALABLE AND RESILIENT SYSTEMS: Building upon the concepts introduced in Book 1, this volume delves into the strategies for designing microservices that are both scalable and resilient. You will learn about essential design patterns and principles, such as bounded contexts, aggregates, and event sourcing, that will help you create systems that can adapt and evolve over time.

BOOK 3 - MASTERING MICROSERVICES: ADVANCED TECHNIQUES FOR OPTIMIZING PERFORMANCE AND SECURITY: In this advanced volume, we explore techniques for optimizing the performance and security of microservices architectures. From performance tuning and caching strategies to security best practices and threat modeling, this book will equip you with the knowledge and skills needed to ensure that your microservices are both fast and secure.

BOOK 4 - MICROSERVICES MASTERY: EXPERT INSIGHTS INTO DEPLOYMENT, MONITORING, AND MAINTENANCE: Finally, in this expert-level volume, we dive deep into the deployment, monitoring, and maintenance of microservices in production environments. You will learn how to automate deployment pipelines, monitor system health, and troubleshoot issues in distributed systems, ensuring that your microservices are always running smoothly.

Whether you're just starting your journey into the world of microservices or looking to take your skills to the next level, "Microservices: Novice to Ninja" has something to offer for every level of expertise. So, buckle up and get ready to become a microservices ninja!

BOOK 1
MICROSERVICES 101
A BEGINNER'S GUIDE TO UNDERSTANDING DISTRIBUTED SYSTEMS

ROB BOTWRIGHT

Chapter 1: Introduction to Microservices Architecture

Microservices, a term that has gained significant traction in recent years within the realm of software architecture, refer to a methodology of designing software systems as a collection of loosely coupled, independently deployable services. These services are organized around specific business functionalities and communicate with each other via well-defined APIs (Application Programming Interfaces). One of the defining characteristics of microservices is their ability to be developed, deployed, and managed independently, allowing for greater agility and scalability in software development processes.

In essence, microservices architecture breaks down complex applications into smaller, more manageable components, each responsible for a specific task or functionality. This decomposition enables teams to work on individual services autonomously, making it easier to scale development efforts and iterate on features without impacting the entire system. Moreover, microservices promote flexibility and resilience by reducing the impact of failures within the system. If one service encounters an issue, it does not necessarily affect the functionality of other services, thus limiting the scope of potential failures and minimizing downtime.

To understand the characteristics of microservices further, let's delve into some of the key principles that define this architectural approach. Firstly, microservices prioritize modularity, with each service encapsulating a single business capability. This modularity allows for easier maintenance, testing, and evolution of individual services without disrupting the entire system. Additionally, microservices advocate for the use of lightweight communication mechanisms, such as HTTP/REST or messaging protocols like AMQP or Kafka, to facilitate interaction between services. This decoupled communication model enables services to evolve independently and promotes interoperability across heterogeneous environments.

Another characteristic of microservices is their emphasis on decentralized data management. Rather than relying on a single, monolithic database, each service typically has its database or data store, optimized for its specific needs. This approach reduces data contention and improves the overall performance and scalability of the system. However, it also introduces challenges related to data consistency and transaction management, which must be carefully addressed through appropriate design patterns and techniques.

In terms of deployment and scaling, microservices offer greater flexibility compared to monolithic architectures. Each service can be independently deployed using containerization technologies like Docker or orchestrated with platforms such as Kubernetes. This allows for more efficient resource utilization and enables organizations to scale individual services based on demand, rather than scaling the entire application stack.

From a development standpoint, microservices promote a culture of autonomy and ownership within development teams. Each team is responsible for the end-to-end lifecycle of the services they develop, from design and implementation to deployment and monitoring. This ownership fosters accountability and empowers teams to make decisions that align with their specific business goals and requirements.

However, it's important to acknowledge that while microservices offer numerous benefits, they also introduce complexities and challenges, particularly in areas such as distributed system debugging, service orchestration, and maintaining consistency across services. Additionally, adopting a microservices architecture requires a cultural shift within organizations, as well as investment in new tools, processes, and infrastructure.

In summary, microservices represent a paradigm shift in software architecture, offering a scalable, flexible approach to building complex applications. By breaking down monolithic systems into smaller, independently deployable services, organizations can achieve greater agility, scalability, and resilience in their software development practices. While adopting microservices requires careful planning and consideration, the potential benefits in terms of speed, scalability, and innovation make it a compelling architectural choice for modern software systems.

Microservices architecture has undergone a remarkable evolution since its inception, driven by the need for scalable, flexible, and resilient software solutions in an increasingly complex and dynamic technological landscape. From its early beginnings as an alternative to monolithic architectures, microservices have evolved to become a foundational paradigm in modern software development practices, enabling organizations to deliver software faster, more efficiently, and with greater agility.

The origins of microservices can be traced back to the early 2000s when software developers and architects began to recognize the limitations of traditional monolithic architectures in the context of rapidly evolving business requirements and technological advancements. Monolithic architectures, characterized by their tight coupling of components and centralized deployment model, often posed challenges in terms of scalability, maintainability, and deployment agility. As applications grew in complexity and scale, it became increasingly clear that a more modular and decentralized approach to software design was needed.

This realization led to the emergence of microservices as an alternative architectural style, drawing inspiration from concepts such as service-oriented architecture (SOA), domain-driven design (DDD), and agile software development methodologies. Microservices architecture advocates for breaking down applications into smaller, loosely coupled services, each responsible for a specific business capability or domain. These services communicate with each other via lightweight protocols such as HTTP or messaging queues, enabling seamless integration and interoperability across distributed environments.

The early adopters of microservices architecture faced numerous challenges, both technical and organizational, as they navigated the transition from monolithic to microservices-based systems. One of the key technical challenges was designing services that were truly independent and encapsulated, with clear boundaries and well-defined interfaces. This required careful consideration of service decomposition strategies, domain modeling techniques, and communication protocols to ensure loose coupling and high cohesion between services.

In addition to technical challenges, organizations also had to grapple with cultural and organizational barriers to adoption. Adopting microservices often necessitated a shift in mindset from centralized control to decentralized autonomy, with development teams taking ownership of individual services throughout the entire software lifecycle. This shift towards DevOps and agile practices, coupled with the adoption of modern tools and technologies for continuous integration, deployment, and monitoring, played a crucial role in enabling organizations to realize the full potential of microservices architecture.

As microservices gained traction in the industry, fueled by success stories from companies like Netflix, Amazon, and Uber, a rich ecosystem of tools, frameworks, and best practices began to emerge to support microservices development and deployment.

Containerization technologies such as Docker revolutionized the way applications were packaged and deployed, providing lightweight, portable environments that could be easily scaled and managed across diverse infrastructure platforms.

Moreover, container orchestration platforms like Kubernetes emerged as a de facto standard for managing containerized workloads at scale, offering features such as service discovery, load balancing, and auto-scaling that were essential for deploying microservices-based applications in production environments. With Kubernetes, organizations could deploy and manage complex microservices architectures with ease, while maintaining high levels of availability, reliability, and scalability.

In parallel to advancements in containerization and orchestration, the microservices ecosystem also saw significant innovation in areas such as service mesh, distributed tracing, and observability. Service mesh technologies like Istio and Linkerd provided a robust infrastructure layer for handling service-to-service communication, traffic management, and security within microservices architectures. Distributed tracing tools such as Jaeger and Zipkin enabled developers to gain insights into the flow of requests across distributed systems, facilitating troubleshooting and performance optimization.

Furthermore, the rise of cloud-native computing and serverless architectures further accelerated the evolution of microservices, offering new paradigms for building and deploying software in a more agile and cost-effective manner. Serverless platforms such as AWS Lambda and Google Cloud Functions abstract away the underlying infrastructure complexities, allowing developers to focus on writing code without worrying about provisioning, scaling, or managing servers.

Looking ahead, the evolution of microservices architecture is poised to continue as organizations embrace emerging technologies such as edge computing, artificial intelligence, and blockchain to drive innovation and competitive advantage. As the complexity of software systems continues to increase, microservices will remain a critical enabler of agility, scalability, and resilience in the digital age, empowering organizations to adapt and thrive in an ever-changing landscape of technological disruption.

Chapter 2: Fundamentals of Distributed Computing

Distributed systems, a fundamental concept in modern computing, encompass a wide range of technologies and architectures designed to solve complex computational problems across multiple interconnected nodes. These systems are characterized by their decentralized nature, where computation, storage, and communication are distributed across a network of interconnected devices rather than being centralized in a single location. Understanding the principles that underpin distributed systems is essential for building robust, scalable, and resilient applications capable of handling the challenges posed by distributed computing environments.

One of the fundamental principles of distributed systems is fault tolerance, which refers to the system's ability to continue operating in the presence of faults or failures. In distributed systems, failures are inevitable due to factors such as hardware malfunctions, network errors, and software bugs. To achieve fault tolerance, distributed systems employ various techniques such as redundancy, replication, and error detection and recovery mechanisms. For example, replication involves maintaining multiple copies of data or services across different nodes to ensure availability and reliability. By detecting and isolating failures and automatically recovering from them, distributed systems can continue operating without significant disruptions to the overall system.

Another key principle of distributed systems is scalability, which refers to the system's ability to handle increasing workloads and accommodate growing numbers of users or requests. Scalability is crucial in distributed systems where resources are distributed across multiple nodes, as it allows the system to maintain performance and responsiveness under varying levels of demand. Horizontal scalability, achieved through techniques such as load balancing and sharding, involves adding more nodes or resources to the system to handle increased traffic or workload. Vertical scalability, on the other hand, involves scaling up individual nodes or resources to handle higher throughput or computational requirements. By designing distributed systems with scalability in mind, organizations can ensure that their applications can grow and adapt to changing business needs and user demands.

Concurrency and consistency are also fundamental principles of distributed systems that govern how data is accessed and manipulated in a concurrent environment. Concurrency refers to the ability of distributed systems to perform multiple tasks or operations simultaneously, allowing for increased throughput and performance. However, concurrency introduces challenges related to data consistency and synchronization, as multiple processes or threads may access and modify shared data concurrently. Distributed systems employ various concurrency control techniques such as locking, transactions, and isolation levels to ensure data consistency and integrity across distributed environments. By managing concurrency effectively, distributed systems can achieve high levels of performance and scalability without sacrificing data consistency or correctness.

Communication and coordination are essential principles of distributed systems that enable nodes to interact and collaborate effectively in a distributed environment. Communication involves the exchange of messages or data between nodes to coordinate their activities and share information. Distributed systems use various communication protocols and mechanisms such as message queues, remote procedure calls (RPC), and publish-subscribe systems to facilitate communication between nodes. Coordination, on the other hand, involves orchestrating the activities of multiple nodes to achieve a common goal or objective. Distributed systems employ coordination techniques such as distributed consensus algorithms, distributed locking, and distributed transactions to ensure that nodes cooperate and synchronize their actions effectively. By enabling seamless communication and coordination between nodes, distributed systems can achieve high levels of efficiency, reliability, and scalability in distributed computing environments.

Resilience and adaptability are additional principles of distributed systems that emphasize the system's ability to withstand and recover from failures and adapt to changing conditions. Resilience involves designing distributed systems with built-in mechanisms for detecting, isolating, and recovering from failures, ensuring that the system can continue operating even in the face of adverse conditions. Adaptability refers to the system's ability to dynamically adjust its behavior or configuration in response to changing environmental conditions or workload patterns. Distributed systems employ techniques such as auto-scaling, self-healing, and dynamic reconfiguration to adapt to varying levels of demand or resource availability. By prioritizing resilience and adaptability, distributed systems can maintain high levels of availability, reliability, and performance in dynamic and unpredictable distributed computing environments.

In summary, understanding the principles of distributed systems is essential for designing, building, and operating robust, scalable, and resilient applications in distributed computing environments. By adhering to principles such as fault tolerance, scalability, concurrency, communication, coordination, resilience, and adaptability, organizations can develop distributed systems that can handle the challenges posed by distributed computing environments and deliver reliable and high-performance services to users. As the demand for distributed computing continues to grow, principles of distributed systems will remain foundational to the design and implementation of modern distributed applications and infrastructure.

Distributed computing, while offering numerous advantages such as scalability, fault tolerance, and resource sharing, presents a unique set of challenges that must be addressed to ensure the successful development, deployment, and operation of distributed systems. These challenges arise from the inherent complexity of distributed environments, where computation, storage, and communication are distributed across multiple nodes connected by a network. Understanding and mitigating these challenges are essential for building robust, reliable, and efficient distributed systems capable of meeting the demands of modern applications and services.

One of the primary challenges in distributed computing is managing consistency and concurrency in a distributed environment. Consistency refers to the requirement that all nodes in a distributed system should have access to the same data at the same time, regardless of where the data is stored or accessed. Achieving consistency in distributed systems is challenging due to factors such as network latency, node failures, and the need for coordination between nodes. Consistency models such as strong consistency, eventual consistency, and causal consistency define the degree to which data consistency is guaranteed in distributed systems. However, implementing and enforcing consistency models in practice requires careful design and implementation of distributed algorithms and protocols.

Concurrency, on the other hand, refers to the ability of distributed systems to perform multiple tasks or operations simultaneously. Concurrency introduces challenges related to data access and manipulation, as multiple processes or threads may access and modify shared data concurrently. Managing concurrency effectively requires the use of concurrency control techniques such as locking, transactions, and isolation levels to ensure data consistency and integrity across distributed environments. However, these techniques often introduce overhead and complexity, impacting the performance and scalability of distributed systems.

Another significant challenge in distributed computing is ensuring fault tolerance and resilience in the face of failures. Distributed systems are prone to various types of failures, including hardware failures, network partitions, and software bugs. Designing distributed systems with built-in mechanisms for fault detection, isolation, and recovery is essential for maintaining system availability and reliability. Techniques such as redundancy, replication, and error detection and recovery mechanisms help mitigate the impact of failures and ensure continuous operation of distributed systems. However, achieving fault tolerance in distributed systems requires careful consideration of trade-offs between performance, consistency, and reliability.

Scalability is another critical challenge in distributed computing, particularly as applications and services grow in complexity and scale. Scalability refers to the ability of distributed systems to handle increasing workloads and accommodate growing numbers of users or requests. Horizontal scalability, achieved through techniques such as load balancing and sharding, involves adding more nodes or resources to the system to handle increased traffic or workload. Vertical scalability, on the other hand, involves scaling up individual nodes or resources to handle higher throughput or computational requirements. Designing distributed systems with scalability in mind requires careful consideration of factors such as data partitioning, resource allocation, and communication overhead to ensure that the system can scale efficiently as demand increases.

Security is another significant challenge in distributed computing, as distributed systems are inherently more susceptible to security threats and attacks compared to centralized systems. Securing distributed systems involves protecting data, communication channels, and access controls against unauthorized access, tampering, and malicious activities. Techniques such as encryption, authentication, and authorization help mitigate security risks in distributed environments. However, securing distributed systems requires a holistic approach that encompasses network security, application security, and data security to ensure comprehensive protection against security threats.

Performance optimization is another challenge in distributed computing, as distributed systems often involve complex interactions between multiple nodes and components. Optimizing performance in distributed systems requires identifying and mitigating bottlenecks, reducing latency, and improving throughput across the system. Techniques such as caching, prefetching, and parallel processing help improve performance by reducing the latency of data access and computation. However, optimizing performance in distributed systems requires careful profiling, monitoring, and tuning of system components to identify and address performance bottlenecks effectively.

Lastly, managing complexity and maintaining system manageability are ongoing challenges in distributed computing. Distributed systems are inherently more complex than centralized systems, as they involve multiple nodes, components, and interactions that must be coordinated and managed effectively. Managing complexity in distributed systems requires the use of design principles, architectural patterns, and tools that promote modularity, abstraction, and encapsulation. Additionally, effective monitoring, logging, and debugging tools are essential for diagnosing and resolving issues in distributed systems. By addressing these challenges, organizations can build and operate distributed systems that are robust, reliable, and efficient, capable of meeting the demands of modern applications and services.

Chapter 3: Understanding Monolithic vs. Microservices Architectures

Monolithic architecture, a traditional software design approach, involves building applications as a single, indivisible unit, where all components and functionalities are tightly coupled and deployed together. In a monolithic architecture, the entire application, including the user interface, business logic, and data access layer, is packaged and deployed as a single executable or deployable unit. This approach contrasts with distributed architectures, where applications are decomposed into smaller, independent services that communicate with each other via well-defined interfaces. Despite the emergence of alternative architectural styles such as microservices and serverless, monolithic architecture remains prevalent in many legacy and enterprise systems due to its simplicity, familiarity, and ease of development.

One of the defining characteristics of monolithic architecture is its centralized and tightly coupled nature, where all components of the application are tightly integrated and depend on each other for functionality. This tight coupling makes it easier to develop and deploy monolithic applications, as developers can work within a single codebase and environment without the need for complex integration or communication mechanisms. Additionally, monolithic architectures typically use a single technology stack or programming language, which simplifies development and reduces the need for cross-team coordination and expertise.

In a monolithic architecture, the application is typically structured as a layered architecture, with distinct layers for presentation, business logic, and data access. The presentation layer is responsible for handling user interactions and rendering the user interface, while the business logic layer contains the core application logic and rules. The data access layer is responsible for interacting with the underlying data storage systems, such as databases or file systems. This layered architecture promotes separation of concerns and modularity, making it easier to understand, maintain, and extend the application over time.

Deployment of monolithic applications is typically done through a single deployment unit, such as a compiled binary or a deployable archive file. The entire application, along with its dependencies and configuration files, is bundled together and deployed to a runtime environment, such as a web server or application server. Deployment of monolithic applications can be done using various deployment tools and techniques, depending on the target environment and deployment requirements. For example, deployment to a web server can be done using tools such as Apache Tomcat or Nginx, while deployment to a cloud platform can be done using platform-specific deployment tools or containerization technologies such as Docker.

Despite its advantages, monolithic architecture also poses several challenges, particularly in terms of scalability, maintainability, and agility. One of the main challenges of monolithic architecture is its limited scalability, as the entire application must be scaled as a single unit. This can lead to inefficiencies and resource wastage, especially in cases where certain components of the application experience higher demand than others. Additionally, monolithic architectures can be challenging to maintain and evolve over time, as changes to one part of the application can have unintended consequences on other parts due to tight coupling and dependencies.

Another challenge of monolithic architecture is its impact on development agility and team autonomy. In a monolithic architecture, development teams often need to coordinate closely and adhere to a single technology stack, which can limit flexibility and innovation. Moreover, deploying changes to monolithic applications can be time-consuming and risky, as any changes to the application require the entire application to be re-deployed, potentially causing downtime and disruption to users. This can hinder the ability of organizations to iterate quickly and respond to changing market demands.

Despite these challenges, monolithic architecture continues to be widely used in many legacy and enterprise systems, particularly in cases where simplicity, familiarity, and ease of development outweigh the drawbacks. Additionally, modern development practices and tools such as continuous integration, continuous delivery, and automated testing have helped alleviate some of the challenges associated with monolithic architecture, enabling organizations to develop and deploy monolithic applications more efficiently and reliably. However, as applications and organizations continue to evolve, there is a growing trend towards alternative architectural styles such as microservices and serverless, which offer greater flexibility, scalability, and agility in the face of changing requirements and environments.

Microservices architecture, a modern software design approach, stands in stark contrast to traditional monolithic architectures, offering a range of distinctive characteristics that differentiate it from its predecessor. At the core of microservices architecture lies the principle of decomposing applications into smaller, loosely coupled services, each responsible for a specific business capability. Unlike monolithic architectures, where all components of the application are tightly integrated and deployed together, microservices architectures promote modularity, flexibility, and scalability by breaking down applications into independently deployable services that communicate with each other via well-defined APIs.

One of the key characteristics of microservices architecture is its emphasis on modularity and service autonomy. In a microservices architecture, each service encapsulates a specific business capability or domain, allowing for clear separation of concerns and modular development. This modularity enables development teams to work on individual services independently, without being constrained by the dependencies and complexities of other services. Moreover, each service in a microservices architecture can be developed, deployed, and scaled independently, providing greater agility and flexibility in the development process.

Another characteristic of microservices architecture is its decentralized and distributed nature. Unlike monolithic architectures, where all components of the application are tightly coupled and deployed together, microservices architectures distribute computation, storage, and communication across multiple services and nodes. This decentralization promotes resilience and fault tolerance by reducing the impact of failures and allowing for graceful degradation in the face of adverse conditions. Additionally, distributed architectures enable organizations to leverage cloud computing and containerization technologies to deploy and manage microservices at scale, across diverse infrastructure platforms.

Scalability is another distinguishing characteristic of microservices architecture, enabling organizations to scale individual services independently based on demand. In a microservices architecture, services can be horizontally scaled by adding more instances or replicas of the service to handle increased workload or traffic. This fine-grained scalability allows organizations to optimize resource utilization and cost-effectively meet the performance requirements of their applications. Moreover, microservices architectures can leverage distributed caching, load balancing, and auto-scaling mechanisms to dynamically adjust resource allocation and handle fluctuating workloads in real-time.

Flexibility and technology diversity are also hallmarks of microservices architecture, allowing organizations to use a diverse range of technologies, programming languages, and frameworks to build and deploy services. Unlike monolithic architectures, which often require developers to adhere to a single technology stack, microservices architectures promote polyglot programming and experimentation with new technologies. This enables organizations to choose the right tool for the job and leverage the strengths of different technologies to address specific requirements or constraints. Additionally, microservices architectures facilitate continuous delivery and deployment practices, allowing organizations to release new features and updates to production rapidly and frequently.

However, despite its advantages, microservices architecture also introduces challenges and complexities that must be addressed to realize its full potential. One of the main challenges of microservices architecture is its inherent complexity, particularly in terms of service discovery, communication, and orchestration. In a microservices architecture, services must be able to discover and communicate with each other dynamically, often across distributed and heterogeneous environments. This requires robust service discovery mechanisms, messaging protocols, and service orchestration tools to ensure seamless integration and interoperability between services.

Another challenge of microservices architecture is managing data consistency and transactionality across distributed services. In a distributed environment, ensuring data consistency and integrity becomes more challenging due to factors such as network latency, partial failures, and eventual consistency. Organizations must implement distributed data management techniques such as distributed transactions, event sourcing, and compensating transactions to maintain data consistency and integrity across distributed services.

Operational complexity is another challenge of microservices architecture, as managing and monitoring a large number of microservices distributed across diverse environments can be challenging. Organizations must invest in robust monitoring, logging, and tracing tools to gain visibility into the performance, availability, and reliability of their microservices. Additionally, organizations must adopt DevOps practices and automation tools to streamline deployment, scaling, and management of microservices at scale.

In summary, microservices architecture offers a range of contrasting characteristics compared to traditional monolithic architectures, including modularity, decentralization, scalability, flexibility, and technology diversity. By breaking down applications into smaller, independently deployable services, microservices architectures enable organizations to achieve greater agility, resilience, and scalability in the development and operation of their software systems. However, adopting microservices architecture also introduces challenges and complexities that must be addressed through careful design, implementation, and management practices. By understanding and mitigating these challenges, organizations can harness the full potential of microservices architecture to build and deploy robust, reliable, and scalable applications in today's fast-paced and dynamic business environment.

Chapter 4: Decomposing Monoliths into Microservices

Breaking down monolithic applications into smaller, more manageable components is a complex and challenging process that requires careful planning, analysis, and execution. However, adopting the right strategies and techniques can help organizations overcome the barriers posed by monolithic architectures and transition towards more agile and scalable software systems. One of the key strategies for breaking down monolithic applications is identifying and defining the boundaries between different functional domains or business capabilities. This involves analyzing the existing monolithic application to identify cohesive modules or components that can be decoupled and extracted into separate services. Domain-driven design (DDD) principles can be helpful in this process, as they emphasize the importance of modeling software systems based on the business domain and identifying bounded contexts where different functionalities can be encapsulated within separate services.

Once the boundaries between different functional domains have been identified, the next step is to decouple and extract these domains into separate services. This process often involves refactoring existing codebase to remove dependencies and create well-defined interfaces between different components. Command-line interface (CLI) tools such as Git can be used to create branches for refactoring and isolating changes, while tools like Docker can be used to containerize individual services and manage their dependencies. Additionally, continuous integration and continuous deployment (CI/CD) pipelines can automate the process of building, testing, and deploying microservices, enabling organizations to iteratively refactor and migrate components of their monolithic application to a microservices architecture.

Another strategy for breaking down monolithic applications is adopting a strangler pattern, where new functionality is developed as microservices alongside existing monolithic codebase. This involves identifying areas of the monolithic application that are candidates for migration to microservices and implementing new features or functionalities as independent services. Over time, as more features are migrated to microservices, the monolithic codebase gradually shrinks, until eventually it is replaced entirely by a collection of microservices. CLI commands such as **git checkout** and **git branch** can be used to create feature branches for developing new functionality, while container orchestration platforms like Kubernetes can be used to manage the deployment and scaling of microservices in production environments.

Additionally, organizations can adopt a modularization strategy to break down monolithic applications into smaller, more modular components. This involves identifying cohesive modules or features within the monolithic codebase and extracting them into separate libraries or modules that can be reused across multiple services. Modularization allows organizations to leverage existing code and functionality while gradually migrating towards a microservices architecture. CLI commands such as **mvn package** or **npm install** can be used to package and publish modular components, while dependency management tools like Maven or npm can be used to manage dependencies between different modules.

Furthermore, organizations can adopt a data-driven approach to breaking down monolithic applications, where data is decoupled from application logic and managed separately by individual microservices. This involves identifying data boundaries within the monolithic application and refactoring data access logic to encapsulate data access within separate services. Tools like Apache Kafka or RabbitMQ can be used to implement asynchronous communication between services, allowing them to exchange data without tight coupling. Additionally, data replication and synchronization techniques such as event sourcing or distributed transactions can be used to maintain data consistency and integrity across distributed services.

Finally, organizations can leverage external APIs and services to break down monolithic applications into smaller, more specialized components. This involves identifying areas of the monolithic application that can be replaced or augmented by third-party APIs or services, such as authentication, payment processing, or content delivery. By outsourcing non-core functionalities to external services, organizations can reduce the complexity of their monolithic application and focus on building core business logic as microservices. CLI commands such as **curl** or **wget** can be used to interact with external APIs, while service mesh technologies like Istio or Linkerd can be used to manage communication and security between microservices and external services.

In summary, breaking down monolithic applications into smaller, more manageable components is a challenging but essential process for organizations looking to adopt more agile and scalable software architectures. By adopting strategies such as identifying functional boundaries, adopting strangler patterns, modularizing codebase, decoupling data, and leveraging external APIs, organizations can successfully transition from monolithic architectures to microservices architectures. However, this process requires careful planning, analysis, and execution to ensure that the benefits of microservices architecture, such as agility, scalability, and resilience, are realized without sacrificing the stability and reliability of existing systems.

Identifying microservices boundaries is a critical aspect of designing and implementing microservices architectures, as it involves determining how to decompose monolithic applications into smaller, independently deployable services that are cohesive and loosely coupled. This process requires careful analysis of the existing monolithic application to identify distinct functional domains or business capabilities that can be encapsulated within separate microservices. One approach to identifying microservices boundaries is domain-driven design (DDD), which emphasizes modeling software systems based on the business domain and identifying bounded contexts where different functionalities can be encapsulated within separate services. Using DDD principles, organizations can analyze the business requirements and domain models of their applications to identify cohesive modules or components that can be decoupled and extracted into separate services. CLI commands such as **git clone** or **svn checkout** can be used to clone the monolithic application's codebase, while tools like Visual Studio Code or IntelliJ IDEA can be used to analyze the code and identify potential boundaries between different functional domains or modules.

Another approach to identifying microservices boundaries is event storming, which involves collaborative workshops where stakeholders map out the business processes and events that occur within the application domain. By visualizing the flow of events and interactions between different components of the system, organizations can identify natural boundaries and seams where microservices can be extracted. During event storming sessions, stakeholders can use whiteboards, sticky notes, and markers to capture and visualize the flow of events and interactions, while facilitators can guide the discussion and ensure that all perspectives are considered. Additionally, tools like Miro or MURAL can be used to facilitate remote event storming sessions and collaborate with distributed teams.

Furthermore, organizations can leverage existing architectural patterns and principles to guide the identification of microservices boundaries. For example, the single responsibility principle (SRP) states that a class or module should have only one reason to change, which can be applied at the service level to ensure that each microservice is responsible for a single, well-defined functionality. Similarly, the bounded context pattern suggests that different parts of a system should have distinct models and terminologies that reflect their specific contexts and boundaries. By applying these principles, organizations can ensure that microservices boundaries are aligned with the underlying business requirements and domain models of the application.

In addition to domain-driven design, event storming, and architectural principles, organizations can also leverage data-driven approaches to identify microservices boundaries. This involves analyzing the data dependencies and access patterns within the monolithic application to identify cohesive modules or components that can be decoupled and extracted into separate services. Tools like database profiling and tracing can be used to monitor and analyze the data access patterns of the monolithic application, while data modeling techniques such as entity-relationship diagrams (ERDs) can be used to visualize the relationships between different data entities and identify potential boundaries.

Moreover, organizations can use metrics-driven approaches to identify microservices boundaries, where key performance indicators (KPIs) and metrics are used to evaluate the cohesion and coupling between different components of the monolithic application. For example, metrics such as code churn, complexity, and coupling can be used to assess the maintainability and scalability of different modules or components, while metrics such as response time, throughput, and error rate can be used to evaluate the performance and reliability of different functionalities. By analyzing these metrics, organizations can identify areas of the monolithic application that are candidates for extraction into separate microservices.

Once potential microservices boundaries have been identified, organizations can validate and refine these boundaries through iterative prototyping and experimentation. This involves implementing lightweight prototypes or proof-of-concept implementations of the proposed microservices to validate their feasibility and assess their impact on the overall system architecture. CLI commands such as **docker-compose up** can be used to spin up lightweight containers for testing and experimentation, while tools like Postman or curl can be used to interact with the prototype services and evaluate their behavior. Additionally, organizations can leverage techniques such as A/B testing and canary releases to gradually roll out the new microservices and collect feedback from users and stakeholders.

In summary, identifying microservices boundaries is a critical step in designing and implementing microservices architectures, as it involves determining how to decompose monolithic applications into smaller, independently deployable services that are cohesive and loosely coupled. By leveraging domain-driven design, event storming, architectural principles, data-driven approaches, and metrics-driven approaches, organizations can identify natural boundaries and seams within their applications where microservices can be extracted. Additionally, by validating and refining these boundaries through iterative prototyping and experimentation, organizations can ensure that the resulting microservices are aligned with the underlying business requirements and domain models of the application, leading to more agile, scalable, and maintainable software systems.

Chapter 5: Communication Patterns in Microservices

Synchronous and asynchronous communication are two fundamental approaches used in distributed systems to exchange information and coordinate interactions between different components or services. Each approach has its own advantages and trade-offs, and the choice between synchronous and asynchronous communication depends on factors such as latency requirements, fault tolerance, and system complexity. Synchronous communication involves a request-response model, where a client sends a request to a server and waits for a response before proceeding with further actions. This approach is commonly used in traditional client-server architectures and web applications, where immediate responses are required to fulfill user requests. CLI commands such as **curl** or **wget** can be used to send synchronous HTTP requests to web servers, while tools like Postman or Insomnia can be used to interact with RESTful APIs and test their responsiveness.

One of the key advantages of synchronous communication is its simplicity and ease of use, as it follows a straightforward request-response pattern that is easy to understand and implement. In synchronous communication, clients can rely on receiving immediate responses from servers, which simplifies error handling and exception management. Additionally, synchronous communication is well-suited for scenarios where strict ordering and consistency are required, as requests and responses are processed in a deterministic and sequential manner. However, synchronous communication can also introduce scalability and reliability challenges, as clients may experience latency or timeouts if servers are busy or unresponsive. Moreover, synchronous communication can lead to tight coupling between clients and servers, making it difficult to scale or evolve the system over time.

In contrast, asynchronous communication decouples the sender and receiver of messages, allowing them to operate independently of each other and asynchronously process messages at their own pace. This approach is commonly used in event-driven architectures and messaging systems, where components communicate through message queues or publish-subscribe channels. CLI commands such as **rabbitmqctl** or **kafka-topics** can be used to manage message queues and topics in message brokers like RabbitMQ or Apache Kafka, while libraries and frameworks like Apache Pulsar or NATS can be used to implement publish-subscribe patterns in distributed systems.

One of the key advantages of asynchronous communication is its scalability and fault tolerance, as it allows components to process messages concurrently and independently of each other. In asynchronous communication, clients can submit requests or messages to a queue or topic and continue with other tasks without waiting for a response. This decoupling of communication allows systems to handle bursts of traffic or spikes in workload more efficiently, as messages can be processed in parallel and asynchronously. Additionally, asynchronous communication promotes loose coupling between components, as senders and receivers are not tightly bound by synchronous interactions. This allows systems to evolve and scale more gracefully over time, as components can be added, removed, or replaced without disrupting the overall system.

However, asynchronous communication also introduces complexity and challenges, particularly in terms of message ordering, reliability, and error handling. In asynchronous communication, messages may be processed out of order or delivered multiple times, leading to potential inconsistencies or race conditions in the system. Moreover, ensuring message reliability and delivery guarantees can be challenging in asynchronous communication, as messages may be lost or delayed due to network failures or system crashes. Organizations must implement robust message processing and error handling mechanisms to ensure that messages are processed reliably and consistently in asynchronous communication.

Additionally, asynchronous communication can introduce challenges in terms of monitoring, debugging, and troubleshooting distributed systems. In synchronous communication, request-response interactions are easy to trace and monitor, as each request corresponds to a single response and follows a linear flow of execution. However, in asynchronous communication, messages may be processed asynchronously and concurrently by multiple components, making it difficult to trace and debug the flow of messages through the system. Organizations must invest in monitoring and tracing tools that provide visibility into the flow of messages and the behavior of distributed components in asynchronous communication.

In summary, synchronous and asynchronous communication are two fundamental approaches used in distributed systems to exchange information and coordinate interactions between different components or services. While synchronous communication follows a request-response model and is well-suited for scenarios where immediate responses are required, asynchronous communication decouples senders and receivers and allows messages to be processed independently and asynchronously. By understanding the advantages and trade-offs of synchronous and asynchronous communication, organizations can choose the most appropriate approach for their specific requirements and design scalable, reliable, and efficient distributed systems.

Event-driven architecture (EDA) is a design pattern that emphasizes the use of events to trigger and communicate changes or actions within a system. In the context of microservices architecture, EDA enables services to communicate asynchronously and decouples the interactions between different components, leading to more flexible, scalable, and resilient systems. One of the key concepts of event-driven architecture is the use of events as first-class citizens, where events represent meaningful occurrences or state changes within the system. Examples of events include user actions, system notifications, or data updates, which are generated by producers and consumed by consumers within the system. CLI commands such as **docker run** can be used to spin up containers running event-driven systems, while event streaming platforms like Apache Kafka or Amazon Kinesis can be used to ingest, process, and distribute events across distributed systems.

In event-driven architecture, events are typically organized and managed using event brokers or message queues, which act as intermediaries for producers and consumers to publish and subscribe to events. Event brokers provide durable storage and delivery guarantees for events, ensuring that events are reliably processed and delivered to consumers even in the event of failures or outages. Moreover, event brokers often support features such as topic-based routing, message replay, and partitioning, which allow organizations to implement sophisticated event-driven workflows and scale their systems horizontally. CLI commands such as **kafka-topics** or **rabbitmqctl** can be used to manage topics and queues in event brokers, while tools like Apache ZooKeeper or etcd can be used to coordinate and manage distributed systems.

One of the key benefits of event-driven architecture in microservices is its ability to decouple services and promote loose coupling between different components. In traditional request-response architectures, services are tightly coupled, and changes to one service can have cascading effects on other services. However, in event-driven architectures, services communicate through events, which allows them to operate independently and asynchronously of each other. This decoupling of communication enables services to evolve and scale more independently, as changes to one service do not necessarily require changes to other services. Moreover, event-driven architecture enables services to react to events in real-time and trigger actions or workflows dynamically based on the occurrence of events.

Another benefit of event-driven architecture in microservices is its ability to handle complex, distributed workflows and business processes more effectively. In event-driven architectures, services can collaborate and coordinate with each other through events, allowing organizations to implement complex event-driven workflows and orchestrations across distributed systems. For example, in an e-commerce application, events such as "order placed," "payment received," and "order shipped" can trigger different actions and updates across multiple services, such as inventory management, billing, and shipping. By leveraging event-driven architecture, organizations can implement resilient, scalable, and fault-tolerant workflows that adapt to changing business requirements and environments.

Moreover, event-driven architecture enables organizations to implement event sourcing and event-driven integration patterns, which can improve data consistency, reliability, and scalability in microservices architectures. Event sourcing involves capturing and storing all changes to the system's state as a sequence of immutable events, which can be replayed and used to reconstruct the system's state at any point in time. This approach enables organizations to implement audit trails, temporal queries, and versioning mechanisms in their systems, leading to more robust and transparent data management. Additionally, event-driven integration patterns such as event aggregation, event transformation, and event routing allow organizations to integrate and synchronize data across disparate systems and services in real-time.

However, event-driven architecture also introduces challenges and complexities that must be addressed to realize its benefits fully. One of the main challenges of event-driven architecture is managing event consistency and ensuring that events are processed reliably and consistently across distributed systems. In event-driven architectures, events may be processed asynchronously and concurrently by multiple consumers, which can lead to potential race conditions, duplicates, or out-of-order processing. Organizations must implement strategies such as idempotent processing, event deduplication, and event replay to ensure that events are processed correctly and consistently.

Additionally, event-driven architectures require organizations to invest in robust event monitoring, logging, and tracing mechanisms to gain visibility into the flow of events and the behavior of distributed components. In event-driven architectures, events are the primary means of communication between services, which makes it essential to monitor and trace the flow of events through the system. By leveraging tools such as distributed tracing systems like Jaeger or Zipkin, organizations can trace the flow of events across distributed services and identify bottlenecks, latency issues, or failures in event processing.

In summary, event-driven architecture plays a crucial role in microservices architectures by enabling services to communicate asynchronously and decoupling the interactions between different components. By leveraging events as first-class citizens and using event brokers to manage and distribute events across distributed systems, organizations can build more flexible, scalable, and resilient systems. However, event-driven architecture also introduces challenges such as event consistency, monitoring, and tracing, which must be addressed to realize its benefits fully.

Chapter 6: Service Discovery and Registration

Service registry patterns play a crucial role in the design and implementation of distributed systems, providing a centralized mechanism for service discovery, registration, and lookup. In microservices architectures, where services are deployed and scaled independently across diverse environments, service registry patterns enable dynamic service discovery and communication, allowing clients to locate and interact with services without hardcoding their locations or endpoints. One of the key service registry patterns is the centralized service registry pattern, where services register their metadata and endpoints with a centralized registry or directory. This approach centralizes service registration and lookup, making it easy for clients to discover and communicate with services by querying the registry. Tools like Netflix Eureka or HashiCorp Consul can be used to implement centralized service registries, allowing services to register themselves with a central server using CLI commands such as **curl** or HTTP clients.

Another service registry pattern is the decentralized service registry pattern, where services use peer-to-peer communication protocols to discover and communicate with each other without relying on a centralized registry. In this pattern, services advertise their presence and endpoints using decentralized protocols such as multicast DNS (mDNS) or peer-to-peer gossip protocols, allowing clients to discover services dynamically without a central point of coordination.

Decentralized service registry patterns are well-suited for dynamic and ephemeral environments, such as edge computing or IoT deployments, where services may come and go frequently and centralized coordination may introduce latency or single points of failure. CLI commands such as **avahi-browse** or **mdns-scan** can be used to discover services advertised via mDNS, while libraries like Serf or SWIM can be used to implement peer-to-peer gossip protocols for service discovery.

Furthermore, hybrid service registry patterns combine elements of both centralized and decentralized approaches, allowing organizations to leverage the benefits of each approach based on their specific requirements and constraints. In hybrid service registry patterns, services may register themselves with both a centralized registry and decentralized discovery mechanisms, providing redundancy and fault tolerance while still benefiting from centralized coordination for service lookup. For example, services may use a centralized registry for service lookup during normal operation but fall back to decentralized discovery mechanisms if the centralized registry becomes unavailable. CLI commands such as **dig** or **nslookup** can be used to query DNS servers and discover services registered via hybrid service registry patterns, while custom scripts or libraries can be used to implement fallback mechanisms for decentralized discovery.

Moreover, service registry patterns can be categorized based on their consistency and availability guarantees, with eventual consistency and eventual availability being common trade-offs in distributed systems. In eventual consistency patterns, service registration and lookup operations may return stale or outdated information due to eventual consistency mechanisms such as eventual consistency protocols or eventual consistency caches. While eventual consistency patterns can improve system availability and fault tolerance by allowing operations to proceed despite network partitions or failures, they may introduce latency or inconsistency in service discovery and communication. In contrast, strong consistency patterns provide strong consistency and availability guarantees for service registration and lookup operations, ensuring that clients always receive up-to-date and accurate information. However, strong consistency patterns may introduce higher latency or lower availability due to the need for coordination and synchronization between distributed components.

Additionally, service registry patterns can be extended to support advanced features such as service health checks, load balancing, and traffic routing, further enhancing the resilience and scalability of distributed systems. For example, service registries can incorporate health checks to monitor the availability and performance of registered services, automatically removing or redirecting traffic from unhealthy services to healthy ones. Similarly, service registries can implement load balancing and traffic routing mechanisms to distribute incoming requests evenly across multiple instances of a service, improving scalability and fault tolerance. CLI commands such as **curl** or **wget** can be used to perform health checks on registered services, while tools like HAProxy or NGINX can be used to implement load balancing and traffic routing at the network level.

Furthermore, service registry patterns can be integrated with service mesh technologies such as Istio or Linkerd to provide additional features such as mutual TLS (mTLS), circuit breaking, and distributed tracing. Service meshes provide a dedicated infrastructure layer for managing and securing service-to-service communication within microservices architectures, allowing organizations to implement advanced networking and security features without modifying application code. By integrating service registry patterns with service mesh technologies, organizations can achieve greater visibility, control, and resilience in their distributed systems. CLI commands such as **istioctl** or **linkerd** can be used to configure and manage service mesh deployments, while observability tools like Jaeger or Zipkin can be used to monitor and trace service-to-service communication.

In summary, service registry patterns are essential building blocks in the design and implementation of distributed systems, providing centralized or decentralized mechanisms for service discovery, registration, and lookup. By leveraging centralized, decentralized, or hybrid service registry patterns, organizations can enable dynamic service discovery and communication in microservices architectures, improving flexibility, scalability, and resilience. Additionally, service registry patterns can be extended to support advanced features such as service health checks, load balancing, and traffic routing, further enhancing the reliability and performance of distributed systems. By understanding the principles and trade-offs of different service registry patterns, organizations can design and implement resilient, scalable, and efficient distributed systems in today's dynamic and heterogeneous computing environments.

Dynamic service discovery mechanisms are fundamental components of modern distributed systems, facilitating the automatic detection and interaction with services in dynamic and ephemeral environments. In distributed architectures like microservices, where services are deployed and scaled dynamically across heterogeneous infrastructure, dynamic service discovery mechanisms enable clients to locate and communicate with services without hardcoded configurations or manual intervention. One of the key dynamic service discovery mechanisms is DNS-based service discovery, which leverages DNS (Domain Name System) to map service names to IP addresses dynamically. In this approach, services register their endpoints with a DNS server using DNS records such as A (Address) or SRV (Service) records, allowing clients to resolve service names to IP addresses dynamically. CLI commands such as **nslookup** or **dig** can be used to query DNS servers and resolve service names to IP addresses, while tools like Consul or CoreDNS can be used to implement DNS-based service discovery in distributed systems.

Another dynamic service discovery mechanism is multicast DNS (mDNS), which enables service discovery in local networks without relying on centralized DNS servers. In mDNS, services advertise their presence and endpoints using multicast messages, allowing clients to discover services dynamically within the same network segment. This approach is well-suited for scenarios where services are deployed in edge environments or IoT (Internet of Things) deployments, where centralized DNS servers may not be available or practical. CLI commands such as **avahi-browse** or **mdns-scan** can be used to discover services advertised via mDNS, while libraries like Avahi or Bonjour can be used to implement mDNS service discovery in embedded systems or IoT devices.

Moreover, dynamic service discovery mechanisms can leverage peer-to-peer communication protocols such as gossip or decentralized registries to enable service discovery in decentralized and distributed environments. In gossip-based service discovery, services exchange information about their endpoints and capabilities with their peers using gossip protocols, allowing each service to maintain a local view of the network topology and discover services dynamically. This approach is well-suited for scenarios where services are deployed across multiple data centers or regions, where centralized registries or DNS servers may introduce latency or single points of failure. CLI commands such as **serf members** or **swim status** can be used to query gossip-based service discovery systems and discover services dynamically, while libraries like Serf or SWIM can be used to implement gossip protocols in distributed systems.

Furthermore, dynamic service discovery mechanisms can be integrated with container orchestration platforms such as Kubernetes or Docker Swarm to enable service discovery and communication in containerized environments. In container orchestration platforms, services are deployed and managed as containers running on a cluster of nodes, and dynamic service discovery mechanisms enable clients to locate and communicate with services running on different nodes within the cluster. Kubernetes, for example, provides built-in service discovery mechanisms using DNS-based service names and environment variables, allowing services to communicate with each other without hardcoded IP addresses or ports. CLI commands such as **kubectl get services** or **docker service ls** can be used to list services deployed on Kubernetes or Docker Swarm clusters, while libraries like Kubernetes Client or Docker SDK can be used to interact with container orchestration platforms programmatically.

Additionally, dynamic service discovery mechanisms can be extended to support advanced features such as service health checks, load balancing, and traffic routing, further enhancing the reliability and scalability of distributed systems. For example, service registries can incorporate health checks to monitor the availability and performance of registered services, automatically removing or redirecting traffic from unhealthy services to healthy ones. Similarly, service registries can implement load balancing and traffic routing mechanisms to distribute incoming requests evenly across multiple instances of a service, improving scalability and fault tolerance. CLI commands such as **curl** or **wget** can be used to perform health checks on registered services, while tools like HAProxy or NGINX can be used to implement load balancing and traffic routing at the network level.

Moreover, dynamic service discovery mechanisms can be integrated with service mesh technologies such as Istio or Linkerd to provide additional features such as mutual TLS (mTLS), circuit breaking, and distributed tracing. Service meshes provide a dedicated infrastructure layer for managing and securing service-to-service communication within microservices architectures, allowing organizations to implement advanced networking and security features without modifying application code. By integrating dynamic service discovery mechanisms with service mesh technologies, organizations can achieve greater visibility, control, and resilience in their distributed systems. CLI commands such as **istioctl** or **linkerd** can be used to configure and manage service mesh deployments, while observability tools like Jaeger or Zipkin can be used to monitor and trace service-to-service communication.

In summary, dynamic service discovery mechanisms play a crucial role in enabling service discovery and communication in modern distributed systems, facilitating automatic detection and interaction with services in dynamic and heterogeneous environments. By leveraging DNS-based service discovery, multicast DNS, peer-to-peer communication protocols, and container orchestration platforms, organizations can build flexible, scalable, and resilient distributed systems that adapt to changing business requirements and environments. Additionally, by extending dynamic service discovery mechanisms to support advanced features such as health checks, load balancing, and traffic routing, organizations can further enhance the reliability and performance of their distributed systems, providing a seamless and consistent experience for clients and users.

Chapter 7: Containerization with Docker

Docker containers have revolutionized the way software is developed, deployed, and managed in modern computing environments. Docker containers provide a lightweight and portable way to package, distribute, and run applications, allowing developers to build and deploy software consistently across different environments. At the heart of Docker containers is the Docker Engine, which is a platform for developing, shipping, and running applications in containers. The Docker Engine consists of several components, including the Docker daemon, which manages container lifecycle operations such as building, running, and stopping containers, and the Docker client, which provides a command-line interface (CLI) for interacting with the Docker daemon. CLI commands such as **docker run**, **docker build**, and **docker stop** are commonly used to manage Docker containers and images, allowing developers to create, deploy, and manage containerized applications with ease.

One of the key benefits of Docker containers is their lightweight and efficient nature, which makes them ideal for microservices architectures and cloud-native applications. Docker containers encapsulate an application and its dependencies into a single, isolated unit, enabling developers to package and distribute applications as immutable artifacts that can be deployed consistently across different environments. Unlike traditional virtual machines (VMs), which require a separate operating system (OS) for each instance, Docker containers share the host OS kernel and only include the necessary libraries and dependencies required to run the application, resulting in smaller, faster, and more efficient deployments. This enables organizations to optimize resource utilization and scale their applications more effectively, reducing infrastructure costs and improving agility.

Another key benefit of Docker containers is their portability and interoperability, which allows developers to build and deploy applications in any environment, from development laptops to production servers and cloud platforms. Docker containers provide a standardized runtime environment that abstracts away differences in underlying infrastructure, enabling developers to build applications once and run them anywhere. This portability is facilitated by Docker images, which are immutable snapshots of a containerized application's filesystem and configuration. Docker images can be easily shared and distributed via container registries such as Docker Hub or private registries, allowing teams to collaborate and deploy applications seamlessly across different environments. CLI commands such as **docker pull** and **docker push** can be used to pull images from and push images to container registries, enabling seamless integration with continuous integration/continuous deployment (CI/CD) pipelines.

Moreover, Docker containers provide a consistent and reproducible environment for developing and testing applications, enabling developers to build, run, and test applications in isolated environments without worrying about compatibility issues or conflicts with other dependencies. Docker containers use a layered filesystem called UnionFS, which allows multiple layers to be stacked on top of each other to create a single, unified view of the filesystem. This enables developers to create lightweight and efficient Docker images by reusing common layers and sharing them across multiple images. Additionally, Docker containers support volume mounts and bind mounts, which allow developers to map directories on the host machine to directories inside the container, enabling seamless integration with development tools and workflows. CLI commands such as **docker build**, **docker run**, and **docker exec** can be used to build, run, and interact with Docker containers during the development and testing process.

Furthermore, Docker containers provide a secure and isolated runtime environment for running applications, protecting them from potential security threats and vulnerabilities. Docker containers use Linux namespaces and control groups (cgroups) to isolate processes, filesystems, network interfaces, and other system resources, ensuring that each container operates in its own sandboxed environment. Additionally, Docker containers support user namespaces and seccomp profiles, which further enhance security by restricting the privileges and capabilities of containerized processes. This enables organizations to implement defense-in-depth security strategies and minimize the attack surface of their applications. Moreover, Docker containers provide built-in support for image signing and verification, enabling organizations to ensure the integrity and authenticity of container images before deploying them in production environments. CLI commands such as **docker inspect** and **docker scan** can be used to inspect container configurations and scan images for security vulnerabilities, enabling organizations to identify and remediate potential security risks.

In addition to these benefits, Docker containers also facilitate efficient resource utilization and scalability, enabling organizations to optimize their infrastructure and scale their applications dynamically in response to changing demand. Docker containers use lightweight isolation mechanisms and shared resources to minimize overhead and maximize resource utilization, enabling organizations to run more containers on the same hardware compared to traditional virtual machines. Moreover, Docker containers support orchestration and clustering frameworks such as Kubernetes, Docker Swarm, and Amazon ECS, which enable organizations to automate the deployment, scaling, and management of containerized applications across distributed environments. These orchestration frameworks provide advanced features such as service discovery, load balancing, rolling updates, and auto-scaling, enabling organizations to build resilient, scalable, and self-healing applications. CLI commands such as **kubectl**, **docker service**, and **ecs-cli** can be used to deploy and manage containerized applications in Kubernetes, Docker Swarm, and Amazon ECS clusters, enabling organizations to leverage the full power of Docker containers in production environments.

Overall, Docker containers have revolutionized the way software is developed, deployed, and managed in modern computing environments, providing developers with a lightweight, portable, and efficient platform for building and running applications. By leveraging Docker containers, organizations can achieve greater agility, scalability, and efficiency in their software development and deployment workflows, enabling them to deliver high-quality applications faster and more reliably. With its rich ecosystem of tools, libraries, and frameworks, Docker continues to drive innovation and transformation in the software industry, empowering developers to build the next generation of cloud-native applications.

Dockerizing microservices applications is a fundamental practice in modern software development, enabling developers to package, deploy, and manage individual microservices as lightweight, portable containers. Docker, an open-source platform, provides a standardized way to encapsulate microservices and their dependencies into self-contained units, known as Docker containers. These containers are isolated from their host environment and contain everything needed to run a microservice, including its code, runtime, libraries, and system tools. Docker containers offer several advantages for microservices applications, including consistency, scalability, and resource efficiency. To begin dockerizing a microservices application, developers typically start by creating a

Dockerfile for each microservice, which contains instructions for building the Docker image. The Dockerfile specifies the base image to use, along with any additional dependencies, configurations, or commands needed to set up the microservice environment. CLI commands such as **docker build** can be used to build Docker images from Dockerfiles, with the **-t** flag specifying the desired tag or name for the image.

Once the Docker images for individual microservices have been built, they can be deployed and orchestrated using container orchestration platforms such as Kubernetes, Docker Swarm, or Amazon ECS. These platforms provide tools and APIs for managing containerized applications at scale, including features such as automatic scaling, load balancing, and service discovery. CLI commands such as **kubectl apply** or **docker service create** can be used to deploy Docker containers to Kubernetes or Docker Swarm clusters, respectively, while configuration files such as Kubernetes Deployment YAMLs or Docker Compose files can be used to define the desired state of the application. Additionally, container orchestration platforms offer built-in support for rolling updates, blue-green deployments, and canary releases, enabling developers to deploy and update microservices applications with minimal downtime and risk.

Furthermore, Docker containers enable developers to achieve consistency and reproducibility across different environments, from development to production. By packaging microservices and their dependencies into

Docker images, developers can ensure that the application behaves consistently across different environments, regardless of differences in underlying infrastructure or configurations. This simplifies the development and testing process, as developers can build and test microservices locally in Docker containers before deploying them to production. CLI commands such as **docker run** can be used to run Docker containers locally on developers' machines, with options such as **-e** for setting environment variables or **-p** for exposing ports. Additionally, tools like Docker Compose can be used to define and manage multi-container applications locally, enabling developers to spin up entire microservices environments with a single command.

Moreover, Docker containers facilitate the modularization and decoupling of microservices applications, allowing developers to break down monolithic applications into smaller, more manageable components. By isolating each microservice in its own container, developers can independently develop, test, deploy, and scale individual services without affecting other parts of the application. This enables teams to adopt agile development practices such as continuous integration and continuous deployment (CI/CD), where changes to microservices can be built, tested, and deployed automatically in response to code changes. CLI commands such as **docker push** can be used to push Docker images to container registries such as Docker Hub or Amazon ECR, while CI/CD pipelines can be configured to trigger Docker builds and deployments in response to code commits or pull requests.

Furthermore, Docker containers provide a lightweight and efficient runtime environment for microservices applications, enabling organizations to maximize resource utilization and reduce infrastructure costs. Unlike virtual machines (VMs), which require a separate operating system kernel for each instance, Docker containers share the host operating system kernel, leading to lower overhead and faster startup times. This allows organizations to run more microservices instances on the same hardware infrastructure, improving scalability and cost-effectiveness. Additionally, Docker containers support resource constraints and limits, allowing organizations to allocate CPU, memory, and storage resources to individual containers based on their requirements. CLI commands such as **docker stats** can be used to monitor resource usage and performance metrics for running Docker containers, while Docker Swarm or Kubernetes can be used to automatically scale containers based on demand.

In summary, dockerizing microservices applications is a key practice in modern software development, enabling developers to package, deploy, and manage individual microservices as lightweight, portable containers. Docker containers offer several advantages for microservices applications, including consistency, scalability, and resource efficiency. By using Dockerfiles to define the build process for microservices images, developers can achieve consistency and reproducibility across different environments. Container orchestration platforms such as Kubernetes or Docker Swarm provide tools for deploying and managing containerized applications at scale, while enabling features such as rolling updates and automatic scaling. Docker containers also facilitate the modularization and decoupling of microservices applications, allowing organizations to adopt agile development practices such as CI/CD. Finally, Docker containers provide a lightweight and efficient runtime environment for microservices applications, enabling organizations to maximize resource utilization and reduce infrastructure costs.

Chapter 8: Orchestration with Kubernetes

Kubernetes, an open-source container orchestration platform originally developed by Google, has become the de facto standard for deploying, managing, and scaling containerized applications in modern cloud-native environments. At its core, Kubernetes provides a flexible and extensible architecture consisting of several key components that work together to automate the deployment, scaling, and management of containerized workloads. Understanding the architecture of Kubernetes is essential for effectively deploying and managing applications on Kubernetes clusters. The Kubernetes architecture is based on a master-slave model, where a cluster consists of one or more master nodes and multiple worker nodes. The master node is responsible for controlling and managing the cluster's state, while the worker nodes execute and run containerized workloads. CLI commands such as **kubectl get nodes** can be used to view the nodes in a Kubernetes cluster, while **kubectl describe node <node-name>** provides detailed information about a specific node.

At the heart of the Kubernetes architecture is the Kubernetes API server, which serves as the central management point for the entire cluster. The API server exposes a RESTful API that clients, including the Kubernetes command-line interface (kubectl) and other Kubernetes components, use to interact with the cluster. CLI commands such as **kubectl get pods** or

kubectl create deployment interact with the Kubernetes API server to perform operations such as querying resources, creating, updating, or deleting objects in the cluster. Additionally, the API server is responsible for validating and authenticating requests, enforcing security policies, and persisting cluster state in etcd, a distributed key-value store.

Another critical component of the Kubernetes architecture is the kube-controller-manager, which runs on the master node and is responsible for managing various controllers that regulate the state of the cluster. Controllers are control loops that continuously monitor the cluster's state and reconcile it with the desired state specified in Kubernetes objects such as pods, deployments, or services. Examples of controllers include the ReplicaSet controller, which ensures the desired number of pod replicas are running, and the Deployment controller, which manages rolling updates and rollback of application deployments. CLI commands such as **kubectl get deployments** or **kubectl rollout status deployment <deployment-name>** can be used to interact with controllers and monitor the status of deployments.

Additionally, the Kubernetes scheduler is a key component responsible for assigning pods to worker nodes based on resource requirements, node capacity, and other constraints. The scheduler watches for newly created pods that have not been assigned to a node and selects an appropriate node for them based on scheduling policies and constraints. The scheduler takes into account factors such as CPU and memory resource requests, node affinity and anti-affinity rules, and pod interdependencies when making scheduling decisions. CLI commands such as **kubectl describe pod <pod-name>** provide insights into the scheduling decisions made by the Kubernetes scheduler.

Furthermore, the kubelet is an essential component that runs on each worker node and is responsible for managing and monitoring the lifecycle of pods. The kubelet receives pod specifications from the Kubernetes API server and ensures that the specified containers are running and healthy on the node. The kubelet interacts with the container runtime, such as Docker or containerd, to create, start, stop, and delete containers as necessary. Additionally, the kubelet performs health checks on pods and reports their status to the Kubernetes API server. CLI commands such as **kubectl get pods** or **kubectl describe pod <pod-name>** provide visibility into the status of pods managed by the kubelet.

Moreover, the Kubernetes networking model enables communication between pods running on different nodes within the cluster. Kubernetes uses a flat, virtual network that spans the entire cluster, allowing pods to communicate with each other using their IP addresses. To achieve this, Kubernetes assigns each pod a unique IP address from the cluster-wide address range and ensures that all nodes can route traffic to and from pods. Additionally, Kubernetes supports various networking plugins and solutions, such as Calico, Flannel, or Cilium, which provide advanced networking features such as network policies, service mesh integration, or encryption. CLI commands such as **kubectl get svc** or **kubectl describe svc <service-name>** can be used to interact with Kubernetes services and expose applications running in pods to external clients.

Furthermore, Kubernetes supports the concept of storage volumes, which allow pods to persist data beyond the lifecycle of individual containers. Kubernetes volumes provide a way to mount storage resources, such as local disks, network-attached storage (NAS), or cloud storage, into pods as directories. Kubernetes supports various types of volumes, including emptyDir, hostPath, persistentVolumeClaim (PVC), and dynamic provisioning with storage classes, allowing developers to choose the appropriate storage solution based on their requirements. CLI commands such as **kubectl get pv** or **kubectl describe pv <pv-name>** can be used to interact with persistent volumes and storage resources in a Kubernetes cluster.

In summary, the Kubernetes architecture consists of several key components that work together to automate the deployment, scaling, and management of containerized applications in modern cloud-native environments. Understanding the role and function of each component is essential for effectively deploying and managing applications on Kubernetes clusters. From the Kubernetes API server to controllers, schedulers, kubelets, networking, and storage, each component plays a critical role in orchestrating and maintaining the state of the cluster. By leveraging the power and flexibility of Kubernetes, organizations can build resilient, scalable, and portable applications that can run anywhere, from on-premises data centers to public clouds.

Kubernetes has emerged as the go-to platform for deploying and managing microservices due to its robust features for container orchestration, scalability, and resilience. With Kubernetes, organizations can effectively deploy, scale, and manage microservices-based applications in dynamic and distributed environments. Deploying microservices with Kubernetes involves several key steps, starting with containerizing individual microservices using Docker or another containerization tool. Once containerized, microservices are deployed to a Kubernetes cluster using Kubernetes manifests, such as YAML or JSON files, which define the desired state of the application. CLI commands such as **kubectl apply -f <yaml-file>** can be used to apply Kubernetes manifests and deploy microservices to the cluster.

Managing microservices with Kubernetes involves various tasks, including scaling, monitoring, and updating microservices to meet changing demand and requirements. Kubernetes provides built-in support for horizontal and vertical scaling of microservices using the Horizontal Pod Autoscaler (HPA) and Vertical Pod Autoscaler (VPA). The HPA automatically scales the number of pod replicas based on CPU or custom metrics, while the VPA adjusts resource requests and limits for individual pods based on observed usage. CLI commands such as **kubectl autoscale** can be used to create an HPA for a microservice, while **kubectl top pods** provides insights into pod resource usage.

Moreover, Kubernetes offers robust monitoring and logging capabilities through integration with monitoring solutions such as Prometheus, Grafana, and Elasticsearch. Prometheus is a popular open-source monitoring system that collects metrics from Kubernetes clusters and microservices, while Grafana provides visualization and alerting capabilities for monitoring data. Elasticsearch, along with its companion tool Kibana, offers centralized logging and log analytics for Kubernetes clusters. Integrating these monitoring and logging solutions with Kubernetes allows organizations to gain insights into the health, performance, and behavior of microservices, enabling proactive monitoring and troubleshooting. CLI commands such as **kubectl port-forward** can be used to access Prometheus, Grafana, or Elasticsearch dashboards locally for monitoring Kubernetes clusters.

Additionally, Kubernetes simplifies the process of updating microservices by supporting rolling updates, blue-green deployments, and canary releases out of the box. Rolling updates allow organizations to update microservices gradually, ensuring zero downtime by gradually replacing old pods with new ones. Blue-green deployments involve deploying a new version of a microservice alongside the existing version and gradually shifting traffic from the old version to the new one. Canary releases enable organizations to test new features or changes by gradually routing a small percentage of traffic to the new version and monitoring its performance. CLI commands such as **kubectl set**

image or **kubectl rollout** can be used to perform rolling updates and manage deployments.

Furthermore, Kubernetes provides robust networking and service discovery capabilities, allowing microservices to communicate with each other seamlessly within the cluster. Kubernetes abstracts networking through the concept of services, which provide a stable endpoint for accessing a set of pods running a microservice. Kubernetes supports various service types, including ClusterIP, NodePort, and LoadBalancer, each with its own use cases and trade-offs. Additionally, Kubernetes offers advanced networking features such as network policies, which enable organizations to define and enforce rules for traffic within the cluster, enhancing security and isolation. CLI commands such as **kubectl expose** can be used to expose microservices as Kubernetes services, while **kubectl describe svc** provides information about service endpoints and configurations.

Moreover, Kubernetes supports stateful microservices through the use of persistent volumes and StatefulSets, allowing organizations to deploy databases, message queues, and other stateful applications in Kubernetes clusters. Persistent volumes provide durable storage for stateful applications, while StatefulSets ensure that pods are uniquely identified and maintain stable network identities across restarts and rescheduling. Kubernetes operators, custom controllers that extend Kubernetes' functionality, provide automation for managing complex, stateful applications, such as databases or messaging systems, in Kubernetes clusters.

CLI commands such as **kubectl create -f <yaml-file>** can be used to create StatefulSets and persistent volume claims for stateful microservices.

In summary, deploying and managing microservices with Kubernetes offers organizations a powerful and flexible platform for building and operating modern, cloud-native applications. With Kubernetes, organizations can easily deploy, scale, and manage microservices-based applications, leveraging features such as automated scaling, rolling updates, advanced networking, and stateful application support. By following best practices and leveraging Kubernetes' extensive ecosystem of tools and integrations, organizations can achieve greater agility, resilience, and efficiency in deploying and managing microservices at scale.

Chapter 9: Testing and Debugging Microservices

Testing microservices presents unique challenges due to their distributed nature, modular architecture, and dependency on external services. To ensure the reliability, performance, and scalability of microservices-based applications, organizations must adopt comprehensive testing strategies that address various aspects of microservices testing. One key strategy is to implement unit testing for individual microservices components to validate their functionality in isolation. Unit tests focus on testing individual units of code, such as functions or methods, to ensure they behave as expected. For microservices, unit tests can be written using testing frameworks such as JUnit, Mockito, or Mocha, depending on the programming language and technology stack used. CLI commands such as **mvn test** or **npm test** can be used to run unit tests for Java or Node.js microservices, respectively.

Additionally, organizations should adopt integration testing to verify the interactions and interfaces between different microservices components. Integration tests validate that microservices communicate correctly with each other, handle data exchange, and maintain consistency across service boundaries. Integration tests can be implemented using tools such as Postman, REST Assured, or Supertest, which allow developers to simulate HTTP requests and verify responses between microservices. CLI commands such as **newman run <collection-file>** or **jest <test-file>** can be used to execute integration tests and validate the interactions between microservices.

Furthermore, contract testing is a crucial strategy for testing microservices interactions and ensuring compatibility between services. Contract testing involves defining and verifying the contracts or agreements between microservices, such as API specifications, message formats, or data schemas. Contract testing tools such as Pact or Spring Cloud Contract enable organizations to define contract tests for microservices APIs and verify that consumers and producers adhere to the specified contracts. CLI commands such as **pact verify** or **./gradlew test** can be used to run contract tests and validate the contracts between microservices.

Moreover, organizations should leverage end-to-end testing to validate the entire microservices-based application from end to end, including all microservices, external dependencies, and user interactions. End-to-end tests simulate real-world user scenarios and verify that the application behaves correctly under different conditions. End-to-end testing frameworks such as Selenium, Cypress, or TestCafe allow organizations to automate user interactions and perform browser-based testing for web applications. For microservices-based applications, end-to-end tests can be implemented to simulate user workflows, API calls, and interactions between microservices. CLI commands such as **npm run test:e2e** or **pytest** can be used to run end-to-end tests for web applications or APIs.

Additionally, organizations should incorporate performance testing into their microservices testing strategy to evaluate the performance, scalability, and responsiveness of microservices under various load conditions. Performance testing tools such as Apache JMeter, Gatling, or Locust enable organizations to simulate concurrent user traffic, measure response times, and identify performance bottlenecks in microservices-based applications. Performance tests can be designed to stress test individual microservices, API endpoints, or entire application workflows to ensure they meet performance requirements. CLI commands such as **jmeter -n -t <test-plan-file>** or **gatling.sh -s <simulation-class>** can be used to run performance tests and analyze the performance metrics of microservices.

Furthermore, organizations should prioritize security testing as part of their microservices testing strategy to identify and mitigate potential security vulnerabilities in microservices-based applications. Security testing encompasses various techniques such as penetration testing, vulnerability scanning, and code analysis to identify security weaknesses and compliance issues. Security testing tools such as OWASP ZAP, Nessus, or SonarQube can be used to perform security scans and audits of microservices code, dependencies, and configurations. CLI commands such as **zap-cli** or **nessuscli** can be used to run security scans and analyze the results for microservices.

Moreover, organizations should adopt chaos engineering as a proactive testing strategy to validate the resilience and fault tolerance of microservices-based applications. Chaos engineering involves deliberately injecting failures and disruptions into a system to observe how it responds and identify weaknesses. Chaos engineering tools such as Chaos Monkey, Gremlin, or LitmusChaos enable organizations to simulate real-world failures and test the resilience of microservices architectures. By introducing chaos experiments such as network failures, latency injections, or instance terminations, organizations can identify weaknesses in microservices deployments and improve their fault tolerance. CLI commands such as **chaos run** or **gremlin attack** can be used to execute chaos experiments and assess the impact on microservices.

In summary, adopting comprehensive testing strategies is essential for ensuring the reliability, performance, and security of microservices-based applications. By combining unit testing, integration testing, contract testing, end-to-end testing, performance testing, security testing, and chaos engineering, organizations can effectively validate the functionality, interactions, scalability, and resilience of microservices architectures. By leveraging a diverse set of testing techniques and tools, organizations can identify and mitigate potential issues early in the development lifecycle, resulting in more robust and reliable microservices-based applications.

Debugging distributed systems poses unique challenges due to their complex and decentralized nature, where components run across multiple nodes, communicate asynchronously, and interact with external services and dependencies. Identifying and resolving issues in distributed systems requires specialized tools, techniques, and strategies tailored to the distributed environment. One of the primary challenges in debugging distributed systems is the lack of visibility into the system's overall state and behavior. With components running on multiple nodes and communicating over the network, traditional debugging tools and techniques may not provide sufficient insight into the interactions and dependencies between components. CLI commands such as **kubectl get pods** or **docker ps** can be used to inspect the state of containers or pods running in a distributed system, providing visibility into the system's components and their status.

Moreover, debugging latency and performance issues in distributed systems can be challenging due to the variability and unpredictability of network communication and resource allocation. Latency spikes, network partitions, and contention for resources can impact the performance of distributed systems, making it difficult to pinpoint the root cause of performance issues. Distributed tracing tools such as Jaeger, Zipkin, or OpenTelemetry enable organizations to trace requests and transactions as they propagate through the system, providing insights into latency, bottlenecks, and dependencies between components. CLI commands such as **kubectl port-forward** or **docker exec** can be used to access tracing dashboards and visualize request flows in distributed systems.

Additionally, debugging consistency and data integrity issues in distributed systems can be challenging due to the eventual consistency model and distributed nature of data storage. With distributed databases and data stores, ensuring consistency and correctness across multiple replicas and partitions is a complex task. Inconsistencies, race conditions, and concurrency issues can arise when multiple components concurrently access and modify shared data, leading to data corruption or inconsistency. Distributed data consistency models such as eventual consistency, strong consistency, or causal consistency provide different trade-offs between consistency, availability, and partition tolerance. CLI commands such as **kubectl exec** or **docker-compose exec** can be used to inspect data stored in distributed databases or data stores and diagnose consistency issues.

Furthermore, debugging failures and errors in distributed systems can be challenging due to their asynchronous and non-deterministic nature. Failures such as node crashes, network partitions, or service outages can occur unpredictably and propagate through the system, leading to cascading failures and service degradation. Distributed systems must be designed to tolerate and recover from failures gracefully, using techniques such as redundancy, replication, and graceful degradation. Additionally, distributed systems monitoring and observability tools such as Prometheus, Grafana, or ELK Stack enable organizations to monitor the health, performance, and availability of distributed systems in real-time, alerting operators to potential issues and failures. CLI commands such as **kubectl logs** or **docker logs** can be used to inspect logs and error messages from containers or pods in distributed systems.

Moreover, debugging security vulnerabilities and breaches in distributed systems is critical for ensuring the confidentiality, integrity, and availability of sensitive data and resources. With distributed systems spanning multiple nodes, networks, and environments, securing communication channels, enforcing access controls, and protecting against attacks such as man-in-the-middle, data breaches, or denial-of-service is essential. Security testing tools such as OWASP ZAP, Nessus, or Qualys enable organizations to scan distributed systems for vulnerabilities, misconfigurations, and compliance issues. Additionally, implementing security best practices such as encryption, authentication, and authorization mechanisms helps mitigate security risks in distributed systems. CLI commands such as **kubectl exec** or **docker-compose exec** can be used to access containers or pods running in distributed systems and perform security assessments.

Furthermore, debugging coordination and synchronization issues in distributed systems can be challenging due to the lack of a global clock and the need for distributed consensus. With distributed systems relying on distributed algorithms such as Paxos, Raft, or gossip protocols for coordination and consensus, ensuring correct and reliable behavior across multiple nodes is essential. Coordination failures, race conditions, and deadlocks can occur when multiple components concurrently access shared resources or coordinate actions, leading to system instability or incorrect behavior. Distributed coordination and consensus libraries such as ZooKeeper, etcd, or Consul provide primitives and abstractions for implementing distributed coordination and consensus protocols in distributed systems. CLI commands such as **kubectl exec** or **docker-compose exec** can be used to interact with coordination and consensus services running in distributed systems and diagnose coordination issues.

In summary, debugging distributed systems presents unique challenges due to their complex, decentralized, and asynchronous nature. Addressing these challenges requires specialized tools, techniques, and strategies tailored to the distributed environment. By leveraging distributed tracing, monitoring, security testing, and coordination tools, organizations can gain insights into the behavior, performance, and security of distributed systems, enabling them to identify and resolve issues effectively. Additionally, implementing best practices such as redundancy, replication, and security measures helps mitigate the impact of failures and vulnerabilities in distributed systems, ensuring their reliability, availability, and security.

Chapter 10: Scaling Microservices for Performance and Resilience

Horizontal and vertical scaling are two fundamental approaches for increasing the capacity and performance of systems, each with its advantages, trade-offs, and use cases. Horizontal scaling, also known as scaling out, involves adding more instances or nodes to a system to distribute the workload across multiple machines. This approach increases the system's capacity and throughput by parallelizing workloads and balancing the load across multiple instances. Horizontal scaling is well-suited for distributed systems and cloud-native architectures, where scalability, resilience, and elasticity are critical requirements. One common example of horizontal scaling is adding more replicas or instances of microservices in a Kubernetes cluster to handle increased traffic or workload. CLI commands such as **kubectl scale deployment <deployment-name> -- replicas=<num-replicas>** can be used to horizontally scale microservices deployments in Kubernetes, increasing the number of pod replicas to distribute the workload.

On the other hand, vertical scaling, also known as scaling up, involves increasing the resources, such as CPU, memory, or storage, of individual instances or nodes in a system to handle increased demand or workload. This approach increases the capacity and performance of a system by upgrading the hardware or provisioning more powerful resources for existing instances. Vertical scaling is suitable for monolithic applications and legacy systems that cannot be easily decomposed into smaller, independent components. For example, increasing the CPU and memory allocation of a virtual machine or database server can improve the performance and capacity of a monolithic application. CLI commands such as **kubectl edit pod <pod-name>** or **docker update --cpus <cpu-count> --memory <memory-size>** can be used to adjust resource allocations for individual pods or containers, enabling vertical scaling in containerized environments.

One of the primary advantages of horizontal scaling is its ability to provide high availability and fault tolerance by distributing workloads across multiple instances or nodes. With horizontal scaling, systems can handle increased traffic or workload without a single point of failure, as failures or outages in individual instances can be mitigated by routing traffic to healthy instances. Additionally, horizontal scaling offers better scalability and elasticity, allowing systems to scale dynamically in response to changes in demand or workload. Cloud platforms such as AWS, Google Cloud Platform, or Azure provide auto-scaling capabilities that automatically adjust the number of instances or nodes based on predefined metrics or thresholds. CLI commands such as **aws autoscaling create-auto-scaling-group** or **gcloud compute instance-groups managed create** can be used to create auto-scaling groups or managed instance groups in cloud environments, enabling horizontal scaling.

However, horizontal scaling also comes with its challenges and trade-offs, including increased complexity in managing distributed systems, data consistency issues, and potential overhead in communication and coordination between instances. Distributed systems must be designed to handle network partitions, data replication, and eventual consistency to ensure correctness and reliability across multiple instances. Additionally, horizontal scaling may require changes to application architecture, such as implementing stateless microservices, distributed caching, or message queues, to fully leverage the benefits of horizontal scaling. Organizations must carefully consider the trade-offs and design considerations when adopting horizontal scaling to ensure optimal performance, scalability, and reliability.

In contrast, vertical scaling offers simplicity and ease of management, as it involves upgrading existing resources without significant changes to the underlying architecture or infrastructure. Vertical scaling is well-suited for applications with predictable workloads or performance requirements, where scaling horizontally may not be cost-effective or feasible. Additionally, vertical scaling can provide better performance improvements for single-threaded or monolithic applications that do not benefit from parallelization or distributed processing. However, vertical scaling has limitations in terms of scalability, as there is a finite limit to the resources that can be provisioned for individual instances or nodes. Eventually, systems may reach the maximum capacity of available resources, leading to performance bottlenecks or scalability limitations.

Moreover, vertical scaling may introduce single points of failure and reduce fault tolerance, as increasing the resources of individual instances does not provide redundancy or resilience against hardware failures or outages. Additionally, vertical scaling may incur higher costs compared to horizontal scaling, as provisioning more powerful resources or upgrading hardware can be expensive, especially for large-scale deployments. Organizations must carefully consider the trade-offs and performance implications of vertical scaling when deciding on scaling strategies for their applications.

In summary, horizontal and vertical scaling are two complementary approaches for increasing the capacity, performance, and resilience of systems, each with its advantages, trade-offs, and use cases. Horizontal scaling offers better scalability, fault tolerance, and elasticity for distributed systems and cloud-native architectures, while vertical scaling provides simplicity, predictability, and performance improvements for monolithic applications and legacy systems. By understanding the characteristics and trade-offs of horizontal and vertical scaling, organizations can choose the appropriate scaling strategy based on their application requirements, performance goals, and scalability needs.

Resilience patterns play a crucial role in ensuring the scalability and reliability of microservices-based applications in dynamic and distributed environments. As microservices architectures rely on numerous interconnected components running across multiple nodes and communicating over the network, they are inherently susceptible to failures and disruptions. Resilience patterns provide techniques and strategies for designing and implementing microservices that can withstand and recover from failures gracefully. One key resilience pattern for microservices scaling is redundancy, which involves deploying multiple instances of a microservice across different nodes or availability zones to ensure high availability and fault tolerance. CLI commands such as **kubectl scale deployment <deployment-name> --replicas=<replica-count>** can be used to scale microservices deployments horizontally by adding or removing replicas.

Additionally, resilience patterns such as graceful degradation and circuit breaker help mitigate the impact of failures and prevent cascading failures in microservices architectures. Graceful degradation involves designing microservices to gracefully handle failures by degrading functionality or providing fallback mechanisms when dependent services or resources are unavailable. Circuit breaker pattern involves implementing a circuit breaker mechanism that monitors the health and responsiveness of downstream services and temporarily opens the circuit to prevent further requests when failures or timeouts occur. CLI commands such as **kubectl exec** or **docker exec** can be used to access containers or pods running microservices and inspect their health and status.

Furthermore, resilience patterns such as retry strategies and timeout mechanisms help improve the robustness and responsiveness of microservices communication.

Retry strategies involve automatically retrying failed requests or operations with exponential backoff and jitter to reduce the impact of transient failures and temporary network glitches. Timeout mechanisms enforce time limits on requests and operations to prevent them from hanging indefinitely and consuming excessive resources. Implementing retry and timeout policies in microservices clients and service invocations helps improve resilience and fault tolerance in microservices architectures. CLI commands such as **kubectl exec** or **docker exec** can be used to access containers or pods running microservices and configure retry and timeout settings.

Moreover, resilience patterns such as bulkhead isolation and throttling help protect microservices from resource exhaustion and overload conditions. Bulkhead isolation involves partitioning and isolating different components or services within a microservices architecture to limit the blast radius of failures and prevent cascading failures from propagating across the system. Throttling involves applying rate limiting and concurrency control mechanisms to regulate the flow of requests and prevent excessive load on downstream services or resources. Implementing bulkhead isolation and throttling mechanisms helps improve the stability and resilience of microservices architectures under heavy load and traffic spikes. CLI commands such as **kubectl exec** or **docker exec** can be used to access containers or pods running microservices and configure bulkhead and throttling settings.

Additionally, resilience patterns such as exponential backoff and jitter help mitigate the impact of congestion and contention in microservices communication. Exponential backoff involves progressively increasing the interval between retry attempts with each consecutive failure to alleviate congestion and reduce the likelihood of collisions and retries. Jitter introduces randomization into retry intervals to prevent synchronized retries and mitigate the thundering herd problem. Implementing exponential backoff and jitter strategies in microservices clients and communication protocols helps improve resilience and reliability in distributed systems. CLI commands such as **kubectl exec** or **docker exec** can be used to access containers or pods running microservices and configure exponential backoff and jitter settings.

Furthermore, resilience patterns such as health checks and self-healing mechanisms help maintain the health and availability of microservices in dynamic and volatile environments. Health checks involve regularly monitoring the health and status of microservices instances and endpoints to detect failures and anomalies proactively. Self-healing mechanisms automatically detect and recover from failures by restarting failed instances, reallocating resources, or rerouting traffic to healthy instances. Implementing health checks and self-healing mechanisms in microservices deployments helps minimize downtime and service disruptions, ensuring continuous availability and reliability. CLI commands such as **kubectl exec** or **docker exec** can be used to access containers or pods running microservices and perform health checks or trigger self-healing actions.

In summary, resilience patterns are essential for ensuring the scalability, reliability, and availability of microservices-based applications in dynamic and distributed environments. By adopting resilience patterns such as redundancy, graceful degradation, circuit breaker, retry strategies, timeout mechanisms, bulkhead isolation, throttling, exponential backoff, jitter, health checks, and self-healing mechanisms, organizations can design and operate resilient microservices architectures that can withstand failures and recover gracefully. CLI commands and container orchestration tools such as Kubernetes or Docker Swarm provide powerful capabilities for implementing and managing resilience patterns in microservices deployments, enabling organizations to build robust and reliable applications at scale.

BOOK 2
ARCHITECTING MICROSERVICES
STRATEGIES FOR DESIGNING SCALABLE AND RESILIENT
SYSTEMS

ROB BOTWRIGHT

Chapter 1: Principles of Scalable and Resilient System Design

Scalability is a fundamental aspect of modern computing architectures, especially in the context of microservices and cloud-native applications where the demand for resources can vary dynamically. Horizontal and vertical scaling are two primary strategies used to address scalability requirements, each with its own advantages and trade-offs. Horizontal scaling, also known as scale-out, involves adding more instances of a component or service to distribute the workload and handle increased demand. In contrast, vertical scaling, also known as scale-up, involves increasing the resources allocated to a single instance, such as CPU, memory, or storage capacity, to handle increased load. CLI commands such as **kubectl scale deployment <deployment-name> --replicas=<replica-count>** or **docker-compose scale <service-name>=<replica-count>** can be used to horizontally scale microservices deployments by adding or removing instances.

Horizontal scaling offers several benefits, including improved fault tolerance, resilience, and performance. By distributing the workload across multiple instances, horizontal scaling reduces the risk of single points of failure and increases the overall availability of the system. Additionally, horizontal scaling can improve performance by leveraging parallelism and concurrency to process requests and tasks more efficiently. Moreover, horizontal scaling provides flexibility and agility, allowing organizations to scale individual components or services independently based on demand. With horizontal scaling, organizations can easily add or remove instances as needed, adapting to fluctuating workload patterns and seasonal variations.

However, horizontal scaling also presents challenges, such as increased complexity in managing distributed systems and maintaining consistency across multiple instances. As the number of instances grows, managing configuration, deployment, and monitoring becomes more challenging, requiring robust automation and orchestration tools. Additionally, ensuring data consistency and synchronization across distributed instances can be complex, especially for stateful applications and shared resources. Moreover, horizontal scaling may incur higher infrastructure costs, as organizations need to provision and manage more resources to support additional instances.

In contrast, vertical scaling offers simplicity and efficiency by scaling up individual instances to meet increased demand. Vertical scaling can be particularly effective for applications with monolithic architectures or single-threaded workloads that cannot be easily parallelized. By increasing the resources allocated to a single instance, vertical scaling can improve performance and capacity without the need for complex distributed systems. CLI commands such as **kubectl scale deployment <deployment-name> --resource-requests=<resource-spec>** or **docker update --memory=<memory-limit> <container-id>** can be used to vertically scale microservices deployments by adjusting resource limits.

Vertical scaling also simplifies management and reduces overhead compared to horizontal scaling, as organizations only need to manage a smaller number of instances. Additionally, vertical scaling can be more cost-effective for certain workloads, as it avoids the overhead of managing and synchronizing multiple instances. However, vertical scaling has limitations in terms of scalability and resilience, as it relies on a single instance to handle all requests and tasks. Moreover, vertical scaling may reach hardware limits or performance bottlenecks, limiting its scalability potential.

In practice, organizations often combine horizontal and vertical scaling strategies to achieve optimal scalability and performance for their applications. This hybrid approach, known as elastic scaling, allows organizations to scale horizontally to handle dynamic fluctuations in demand and vertically to address performance bottlenecks or resource constraints. By leveraging both horizontal and vertical scaling, organizations can achieve the flexibility, resilience, and efficiency required to support modern cloud-native applications. CLI commands such as **kubectl autoscale deployment <deployment-name> --min=<min-replicas> --max=<max-replicas>** or **docker-compose scale <service-name>=<replica-count>** can be used to implement elastic scaling strategies in microservices deployments.

Overall, scalability is a critical consideration for designing and deploying microservices-based applications, and both horizontal and vertical scaling strategies play important roles in achieving scalability goals. By understanding the strengths and limitations of each scaling approach and leveraging automation and orchestration tools, organizations can build resilient, efficient, and scalable architectures that can adapt to changing business requirements and workload patterns. Resilience is a critical aspect of designing and operating distributed systems, ensuring that applications can continue to function in the face of failures and disruptions. Redundancy and failover mechanisms are key components of resilience strategies, providing redundancy and fault tolerance to mitigate the impact of failures on system availability and reliability. Redundancy involves duplicating critical components, data, or resources within a system to ensure that alternative resources are available in case of failure. CLI commands such as **kubectl scale deployment <deployment-name> --replicas=<replica-count>** or **docker-compose scale <service-name>=<replica-count>** can be used to deploy redundant instances of microservices to distribute workload and increase fault tolerance.

Redundancy can be implemented at various levels of the technology stack, including hardware, software, and data storage. At the hardware level, redundancy can be achieved through techniques such as disk mirroring, RAID (Redundant Array of Independent Disks), or hot standby servers. Disk mirroring involves duplicating data across multiple disks to ensure that data remains accessible in case of disk failure. RAID configurations combine multiple disks into a single logical unit to improve performance and redundancy. Hot standby servers are redundant servers that remain idle until they are needed to take over operations in case of primary server failure.

At the software level, redundancy can be implemented through techniques such as load balancing, clustering, and replication. Load balancing distributes incoming requests across multiple servers to evenly distribute workload and prevent overload on individual servers. Clustering involves grouping multiple servers together to share resources and provide high availability and fault tolerance. Replication involves duplicating data across multiple servers or data centers to ensure data availability and integrity in case of server or data center failure.

Moreover, redundancy can be implemented at the data storage level through techniques such as data replication, sharding, and backups. Data replication involves synchronously or asynchronously copying data across multiple storage devices or data centers to ensure data availability and durability. Sharding involves partitioning data into smaller subsets and distributing them across multiple servers to improve performance and scalability. Backups involve regularly creating copies of data and storing them in a separate location to protect against data loss due to hardware failure, corruption, or malicious activity.

Failover mechanisms complement redundancy by automatically detecting and responding to failures to ensure uninterrupted service availability. Failover mechanisms involve transferring operations from a failed component to a redundant or standby component to maintain service continuity. CLI commands such as **kubectl get pods** or **docker service ls** can be used to monitor the health and status of microservices instances, while tools like Kubernetes or Docker Swarm can automate failover processes.

Failover mechanisms can be implemented at various levels of the system, including network, application, and data layers. Network-level failover mechanisms involve rerouting traffic from a failed network path to an alternative path to ensure continuous connectivity. Application-level failover mechanisms involve redirecting requests from a failed application instance to a redundant instance to maintain service availability. Data-level failover mechanisms involve switching from a failed database server to a standby server to ensure data availability and integrity.

Furthermore, failover mechanisms can be proactive or reactive in nature. Proactive failover mechanisms anticipate and preemptively respond to potential failures based on predefined conditions or thresholds. Reactive failover mechanisms detect failures after they occur and initiate failover processes to restore service availability. Implementing a combination of proactive and reactive failover mechanisms helps ensure timely and effective response to failures and disruptions.

Additionally, failover mechanisms can be manual or automated depending on the level of autonomy and control desired. Manual failover mechanisms require human intervention to initiate failover processes, while automated failover mechanisms rely on predefined rules and algorithms to automatically detect and respond to failures. Automated failover mechanisms are typically faster and more reliable than manual failover mechanisms, as they can respond to failures immediately without human intervention.

In summary, resilience strategies such as redundancy and failover mechanisms are essential for ensuring the availability, reliability, and continuity of distributed systems. By implementing redundancy at various levels of the technology stack and deploying failover mechanisms to automatically respond to failures, organizations can minimize downtime, prevent data loss, and maintain service availability in the face of failures and disruptions. CLI commands and orchestration tools provide powerful capabilities for deploying and managing redundant instances of microservices and automating failover processes, enabling organizations to build resilient and reliable distributed systems.

Chapter 2: Domain-Driven Design for Microservices

In domain-driven design (DDD), bounded contexts and ubiquitous language are fundamental concepts that play a crucial role in defining and modeling complex business domains. Bounded contexts represent specific areas or boundaries within a domain where a particular model and set of concepts apply consistently. They help delineate different aspects of the domain and establish clear boundaries between different subdomains or business functionalities. CLI commands such as **kubectl get pods** or **docker ps** can be used to inspect the status of microservices instances running within bounded contexts.

Within each bounded context, the concept of ubiquitous language is employed to establish a shared understanding and vocabulary among stakeholders, domain experts, and development teams. Ubiquitous language consists of a set of terms and concepts that are consistent and meaningful within the context of the domain. These terms are used consistently across different parts of the system, facilitating communication and collaboration among team members and ensuring alignment between business requirements and software implementation.

The concept of bounded contexts is closely related to the principles of encapsulation and modularization in software design. By defining clear boundaries around specific areas of the domain, bounded contexts enable teams to focus on developing models and functionalities that are relevant to their respective contexts without being encumbered by concerns from other parts of the domain. This encapsulation fosters modularity, flexibility, and scalability in the design and implementation of complex systems.

Moreover, bounded contexts help address the challenges of complexity and ambiguity that often arise in large-scale software projects. By breaking down the domain into smaller, more manageable contexts, teams can better understand and reason about the domain, leading to more effective communication, collaboration, and decision-making. CLI commands such as **kubectl describe pod <pod-name>** or **docker inspect <container-id>** can be used to obtain detailed information about microservices instances and their configurations within bounded contexts.

Additionally, bounded contexts provide a natural alignment between domain experts and development teams, as each team can take ownership of a specific bounded context and develop a model and implementation that accurately reflects the requirements and constraints of that context. This alignment helps reduce the risk of miscommunication, misunderstanding, and misalignment between stakeholders and development teams, leading to more successful and resilient software projects.

Furthermore, bounded contexts enable teams to evolve and iterate on their models and implementations independently without impacting other parts of the system. This autonomy allows teams to innovate, experiment, and adapt to changing requirements and business needs within their respective contexts. CLI commands such as **kubectl apply -f <deployment-file>** or **docker-compose up -d** can be used to deploy microservices instances within bounded contexts, enabling teams to test and iterate on their implementations in isolation.

However, managing interactions and dependencies between bounded contexts can pose challenges, particularly in distributed systems where different contexts may need to communicate and collaborate with each other. In such cases, it is essential to define clear interfaces and communication protocols between bounded contexts to ensure interoperability and consistency across the system. CLI commands such as **kubectl exec -it <pod-name> -- /bin/bash** or **docker exec -it <container-id> /bin/bash** can be used to access microservices instances within bounded contexts and debug interactions between them.

Moreover, as the complexity and scale of software projects increase, it is important to establish mechanisms for coordinating and integrating changes across bounded contexts. Continuous integration and continuous deployment (CI/CD) pipelines can help automate the process of building, testing, and deploying changes to bounded contexts, ensuring that updates are rolled out smoothly and consistently across the system. CLI commands such as **kubectl rollout restart deployment <deployment-name>** or **docker-compose restart <service-name>** can be used to trigger rolling updates of microservices instances within bounded contexts.

In summary, bounded contexts and ubiquitous language are essential concepts in domain-driven design that help teams effectively model, communicate, and implement complex business domains. By defining clear boundaries around specific areas of the domain and establishing a shared vocabulary and understanding, teams can better align their software solutions with business requirements and achieve greater success in delivering resilient and scalable systems. CLI commands and automation tools play a key role in deploying, managing, and evolving microservices instances within bounded contexts, enabling teams to build and maintain complex distributed systems effectively.

In domain-driven design (DDD), aggregates, entities, and value objects are key building blocks used to model and represent domain concepts and relationships within a software system. These concepts help developers organize and structure domain logic in a way that reflects the business requirements and constraints of the domain. Aggregates are clusters of domain objects that are treated as a single unit for data consistency and transactional integrity. An aggregate typically consists of a root entity, which serves as the primary access point to the aggregate, along with one or more associated entities and value objects. CLI commands such as **kubectl apply -f <deployment-file>** or **docker-compose up -d** can be used to deploy microservices instances that represent aggregates within a bounded context.

Entities are objects that have a distinct identity and lifecycle within the domain. They represent real-world entities such as customers, orders, or products and encapsulate both state and behavior related to their identity. Entities are typically mutable and are often the focal point of domain logic and business rules. Value objects, on the other hand, are immutable objects that represent attributes or characteristics of domain entities. They are used to model concepts such as dates, quantities, or addresses and are often composed of multiple attributes. Value objects are immutable to ensure data consistency and prevent unintended side effects.

The distinction between entities and value objects lies in their identity and mutability. Entities have a unique identity that persists over time and can be distinguished based on their identity attributes. Changes to an entity's state are reflected in the entity itself, and entities are typically stored and retrieved from a persistent data store using their identity. Value objects, on the other hand, are identified based on their attribute values rather than a unique identity. Since value objects are immutable, changes to their state result in the creation of a new value object with updated attribute values.

Aggregates serve as a mechanism for encapsulating and managing consistency boundaries within the domain. By grouping related entities and value objects together within an aggregate, developers can define clear transactional boundaries and ensure data consistency and integrity. Operations on aggregates are typically performed atomically, meaning that changes to one part of the aggregate either succeed or fail together. This ensures that the aggregate remains in a valid and consistent state at all times. CLI commands such as

kubectl exec -it <pod-name> -- /bin/bash or **docker exec -it <container-id> /bin/bash** can be used to access microservices instances representing aggregates and perform operations within the aggregate.

Moreover, aggregates help enforce business rules and constraints by encapsulating domain logic within the aggregate boundaries. By defining behavior and operations on aggregates, developers can ensure that business rules are consistently applied and enforced across the system. Aggregates also serve as a natural unit of consistency and concurrency control, allowing multiple users or processes to work with different aggregates concurrently without interfering with each other. This helps improve performance and scalability in distributed systems.

Entities and value objects play complementary roles within aggregates, with entities representing the primary actors or subjects within the domain and value objects representing the attributes or characteristics associated with those entities. Entities encapsulate identity and behavior, while value objects encapsulate attributes and characteristics. CLI commands such as **kubectl describe pod <pod-name>** or **docker inspect <container-id>** can be used to obtain detailed information about microservices instances representing entities and value objects within aggregates.

Furthermore, entities and value objects can have complex relationships and dependencies within aggregates. Entities may reference other entities or value objects within the same aggregate or across different aggregates. Value objects may be shared and reused across multiple entities or aggregates to represent common attributes or concepts. By carefully defining relationships and dependencies between entities and value objects, developers can create flexible and expressive domain models that accurately reflect the complexities of the business domain.

In summary, aggregates, entities, and value objects are essential concepts in domain-driven design that help developers model and represent complex business domains in software systems. By grouping related domain objects together within aggregates and defining clear boundaries and relationships, developers can create cohesive and expressive domain models that align closely with business requirements and constraints. CLI commands and container orchestration tools provide powerful capabilities for deploying, managing, and interacting with microservices instances representing aggregates, entities, and value objects within bounded contexts, enabling developers to build robust and scalable systems effectively.

Chapter 3: Event-Driven Architecture and Asynchronous Communication

Event Sourcing and Command Query Responsibility Segregation (CQRS) are architectural patterns that address the challenges of designing and implementing scalable, resilient, and maintainable systems, especially in the context of complex distributed applications. Event Sourcing is a pattern where the state of a system is determined by a sequence of events, rather than the current state. Each event represents a state change in the system and is stored as an immutable record in an event log. CLI commands such as **kubectl apply -f <deployment-file>** or **docker-compose up -d** can be used to deploy microservices instances that implement event sourcing.

In Event Sourcing, instead of directly modifying the state of an entity, commands are processed and translated into events that capture the intention and outcome of the command. These events are then appended to the event log, which serves as the source of truth for the system's state. By storing events as immutable records, Event Sourcing provides a reliable audit trail of all changes to the system's state, enabling developers to track and analyze the history of the system and diagnose issues more effectively.

Moreover, Event Sourcing enables developers to implement complex business logic and workflows by replaying events and projecting them into different views or representations of the system's state. This allows developers to derive insights, generate reports, or implement new features without modifying the underlying event log. CLI commands such as **kubectl exec -it <pod-name> -- /bin/bash** or **docker exec -it <container-id> /bin/bash** can be used to access microservices instances that implement event sourcing and perform operations on the event log.

CQRS, on the other hand, is a pattern that separates the responsibility for handling commands (write operations) from queries (read operations) in a system. In a traditional CRUD (Create, Read, Update, Delete) model, a single data model is used to handle both commands and queries, which can lead to complexity and performance issues as the system scales. CQRS addresses this by introducing separate read and write models, each optimized for its respective use case.

In CQRS, commands are processed by a command handler, which validates and executes the command, producing one or more events that represent the outcome of the command. These events are then appended to the event log using Event Sourcing. Meanwhile, queries are handled by query handlers, which read data from one or more read models optimized for querying and reporting. By separating commands and queries, CQRS enables developers to optimize the system for different access patterns and scalability requirements.

Furthermore, CQRS allows developers to scale and evolve the read and write sides of the system independently. For example, the read model can be denormalized and optimized for fast read access, while the write model can be optimized for efficient event processing and storage. This separation of concerns simplifies the design and implementation of complex systems and allows developers to adapt the system to changing requirements and performance constraints more easily.

Additionally, Event Sourcing and CQRS complement each other and are often used together to build scalable and resilient systems. By combining Event Sourcing with CQRS, developers can leverage the benefits of both patterns to achieve greater flexibility, scalability, and maintainability in their applications. CLI commands such as **kubectl apply -f <deployment-file>** or **docker-compose up -d** can be used to deploy microservices instances that implement both Event Sourcing and CQRS.

In summary, Event Sourcing and CQRS are powerful architectural patterns that address the challenges of designing and implementing complex distributed systems. Event Sourcing provides a reliable and auditable mechanism for capturing and storing the history of a system's state, while CQRS enables developers to separate commands and queries, optimizing the system for different access patterns and scalability requirements. By combining Event Sourcing with CQRS, developers can build scalable, resilient, and maintainable systems that can adapt to changing business requirements and performance constraints effectively.

Message brokers play a crucial role in modern distributed systems by facilitating communication and data exchange between different components and services. They act as intermediaries that receive, store, and deliver messages between producers and consumers, enabling asynchronous and decoupled communication patterns. Kafka and RabbitMQ are two popular message brokers widely used in the industry, each offering unique features and capabilities suited for different use cases. Deploying and managing message brokers such as Kafka or RabbitMQ requires careful consideration of factors such as scalability, reliability, and performance. For example, to deploy Kafka, one can use Docker Compose to define and run a multi-container Docker application consisting of Kafka brokers, ZooKeeper, and other required components. The Docker Compose configuration file specifies the services, networks, and volumes needed for the Kafka deployment, allowing developers to easily spin up Kafka clusters for development, testing, or production environments. Similarly, RabbitMQ can be deployed using Docker containers, with Docker Compose providing a convenient way to define and manage RabbitMQ instances along with any necessary dependencies such as databases or monitoring tools. Once deployed, Kafka and RabbitMQ offer powerful features for message queuing, pub/sub messaging, and stream processing, enabling developers to build scalable, resilient, and event-driven systems. Kafka, for example, excels at handling high-throughput, fault-tolerant message streams, making it ideal for use cases such as log aggregation, event sourcing, and real-time analytics. RabbitMQ, on the other hand, specializes in supporting various messaging patterns such as point-to-point, publish/subscribe, and request/reply, making it well-suited for applications requiring flexible and reliable message routing. Both Kafka and RabbitMQ provide client libraries and APIs for popular programming languages such as Java, Python, and JavaScript, allowing developers to integrate message brokers seamlessly into their applications. These client libraries offer features for producing and consuming messages, managing message queues, and handling message acknowledgments, ensuring robust and efficient communication between services. Additionally, Kafka and RabbitMQ offer advanced features such as message batching, message compression, and message partitioning, allowing developers to optimize message throughput, latency, and resource utilization. Monitoring and management tools such as Kafka Manager, Burrow, and RabbitMQ Management UI provide insights into the health, performance, and activity of Kafka and RabbitMQ clusters, enabling administrators to monitor resource usage, track message throughput, and troubleshoot issues effectively. CLI commands such as **docker-compose up -d** or **docker-compose logs <service-name>** can be used to deploy and manage Kafka or RabbitMQ instances running in Docker containers, while tools like Kafka Manager or RabbitMQ Management UI offer web-based interfaces for monitoring and managing message brokers. In summary, Kafka, RabbitMQ, and other message brokers are essential components of modern distributed systems, providing reliable and scalable messaging infrastructure for building event-driven architectures, microservices, and real-time data pipelines. By leveraging message brokers such as Kafka and RabbitMQ, developers can decouple services, handle high-volume message streams, and build resilient and responsive applications that meet the demands of today's distributed environments.

Chapter 4: Data Management Strategies in Microservices

Polyglot persistence is a strategy in database architecture where multiple data storage technologies are used to handle different types of data within a single application or system. This approach recognizes that different data models and access patterns may require different storage solutions, and aims to select the most appropriate data store for each use case. CLI commands such as docker run or kubectl apply -f can be used to deploy various data stores, depending on the chosen technology and deployment environment. When designing a polyglot persistence strategy, it is essential to understand the characteristics and requirements of the data being stored, as well as the strengths and weaknesses of different storage technologies. For example, relational databases such as PostgreSQL or MySQL are well-suited for structured data with complex relationships and transactions, making them suitable for use cases such as e-commerce, finance, and inventory management. To deploy a relational database like PostgreSQL using Docker, one can use the docker run command to create a containerized instance of PostgreSQL, specifying parameters such as the database name, username, and password. NoSQL databases such as MongoDB or Cassandra, on the other hand, are designed for handling unstructured or semi-structured data with flexible schemas, making them suitable for use cases such as content management, IoT data processing, and real-time analytics. Deploying MongoDB using Docker involves running a containerized instance of MongoDB using the docker run command, specifying parameters such as the data volume and network settings. In addition to relational and NoSQL databases, polyglot persistence may also involve using specialized data stores for specific use cases, such as graph databases like Neo4j for modeling complex relationships, time-series databases like InfluxDB for storing and querying time-series data, or key-value stores like Redis for caching and high-speed data access. Each of these data stores offers unique features and capabilities that make them suitable for different types of data and access patterns. When deploying specialized data stores like Neo4j or InfluxDB, it is important to configure the containerized instances according to the specific requirements of the application, such as setting up replication, sharding, or clustering for high availability and fault tolerance. Another consideration when implementing polyglot persistence is data synchronization and consistency across multiple data stores. Since each data store may have its own data model and consistency guarantees, maintaining consistency between different stores can be challenging. Solutions such as event sourcing, data replication, or distributed transactions may be used to synchronize data between different stores and ensure consistency across the system. When deploying data synchronization mechanisms, it is important to consider factors such as latency, throughput, and data consistency guarantees to ensure that the system meets its performance and reliability requirements. Monitoring and management tools such as Prometheus, Grafana, or DataDog can be used to monitor the health, performance, and activity of polyglot persistence deployments, providing insights into resource usage, query performance, and data consistency. By monitoring key metrics such as CPU utilization, memory usage, and disk I/O, administrators can identify bottlenecks, optimize resource allocation, and troubleshoot issues to ensure the reliability and scalability of polyglot persistence deployments. In summary, polyglot persistence offers a flexible and scalable approach to data storage and management, allowing developers to select the most appropriate data stores for each use case within a single application or system. By leveraging a combination of relational databases, NoSQL databases, and specialized data stores, organizations can meet the diverse requirements of modern applications, from handling structured transactional data to processing unstructured or time-series data at scale. CLI commands and container orchestration tools provide convenient ways to deploy and manage polyglot persistence deployments, enabling developers to build resilient, high-performance applications that leverage the strengths of different data storage technologies. Maintaining data consistency in a microservices architecture presents unique challenges due to the distributed nature of the system. Various data consistency patterns have emerged to address these challenges and ensure that data remains accurate and up-to-date across multiple microservices.

One such pattern is the Saga pattern, which orchestrates a series of compensating transactions to maintain consistency across multiple microservices. CLI commands such as docker run or kubectl apply -f can be used to deploy microservices instances implementing the Saga pattern. In the Saga pattern, a long-running transaction is divided into a series of smaller, loosely coupled transactions, each executed within the context of a single microservice. If a transaction fails, compensating transactions are executed to undo the changes made by previous transactions and restore the system to a consistent state. Another data consistency pattern is the Event Sourcing pattern, which captures all changes to the system's state as a sequence of immutable events. CLI commands such as docker-compose up -d or kubectl exec -it <pod-name> -- /bin/bash can be used to deploy microservices instances that implement Event Sourcing. In Event Sourcing, events are stored as immutable records in an event log, providing a reliable audit trail of all changes to the system's state. By replaying events, developers can rebuild the system's state at any point in time, ensuring data consistency and enabling features such as auditing, debugging, and analytics. Additionally, the CQRS (Command Query Responsibility Segregation) pattern complements Event Sourcing by separating commands that modify the system's state from queries that retrieve data from the system. CLI commands such as docker exec -it <container-id> /bin/bash or kubectl describe pod <pod-name> can be used to access microservices instances implementing CQRS. With

CQRS, developers can optimize the read and write sides of the system independently, allowing for improved performance, scalability, and flexibility. The Materialized View pattern is another data consistency pattern that precomputes and caches query results to improve read performance and reduce latency. CLI commands such as docker-compose logs <service-name> or kubectl logs <pod-name> can be used to monitor and troubleshoot microservices instances implementing Materialized Views. By maintaining separate materialized views for different query patterns, developers can optimize the system for specific access patterns and improve overall performance. However, achieving data consistency in a microservices architecture requires careful consideration of factors such as latency, throughput, and fault tolerance. Solutions such as distributed transactions, eventual consistency, and consensus algorithms may be used to ensure data consistency and reliability across microservices. CLI commands such as docker inspect <container-id> or kubectl describe pod <pod-name> can be used to gather information about the runtime environment and configuration of microservices instances. Moreover, monitoring and management tools such as Prometheus, Grafana, or DataDog provide insights into the health, performance, and activity of microservices deployments, enabling administrators to identify and troubleshoot data consistency issues effectively. In summary, data consistency patterns play a crucial role in ensuring the reliability and integrity of data in a microservices architecture. By leveraging patterns such as Saga, Event Sourcing, CQRS, and Materialized Views, developers can address the challenges of distributed data management and build resilient, scalable, and maintainable microservices-based systems.CLI commands and container orchestration tools provide convenient ways to deploy and manage microservices instances implementing data consistency patterns, enabling developers to build robust and reliable systems effectively.

Chapter 5: Service Choreography vs. Orchestration

In the realm of microservices architecture, choreography serves as a decentralized communication pattern that allows individual services to interact autonomously without relying on a central orchestrator. This approach contrasts with the more traditional orchestration pattern, where a central component dictates the flow of communication between services. In choreography, services communicate directly with one another, exchanging messages to coordinate actions and achieve desired outcomes. The decentralized nature of choreography offers benefits such as increased scalability, flexibility, and resilience, as services can evolve independently and adapt to changing requirements without introducing dependencies on a central orchestrator. Deploying choreography-based communication in a microservices architecture often involves using message brokers or event-driven systems to facilitate message exchange between services. Tools such as Apache Kafka or RabbitMQ can be deployed using CLI commands like **docker run** or **kubectl apply -f** to set up message queues or topics for communication between services. Once deployed, services can publish messages to these queues or topics to notify other services of relevant events or actions. Moreover, choreography encourages loose coupling between services, as each service only needs to be aware of the messages it sends and receives, rather than the entire communication flow of the system. This loose coupling enables services to evolve independently, making it easier to maintain and scale the system over time. Additionally, choreography fosters resilience in distributed systems by distributing responsibility for handling communication among services. If one service becomes unavailable or experiences issues, other services can continue to operate independently, reducing the impact of failures on the system as a whole. However, implementing choreography-based communication also comes with challenges, particularly around managing the complexity of message flows and ensuring consistency and reliability in message exchange. Tools such as circuit breakers, retries, and dead-letter queues can help mitigate these challenges by providing mechanisms for handling errors and recovering from failures gracefully. Deploying these resilience patterns often involves configuring libraries or frameworks used by services to handle message processing and communication. For example, libraries like Hystrix or resilience4j can be integrated into microservices using build tools such as Maven or Gradle, with dependencies specified in the project's configuration files. Furthermore, monitoring and observability are essential aspects of managing choreography-based communication in microservices architectures. Tools such as Prometheus, Grafana, or ELK stack can be deployed using CLI commands like **helm install** or **kubectl apply -f** to monitor the health, performance, and activity of services and message brokers. By collecting and analyzing metrics and logs generated by services and message brokers, operators can gain insights into the behavior of the system and identify potential issues or bottlenecks. Additionally, distributed tracing tools like Jaeger or Zipkin can be deployed to trace the flow of messages through the system, helping to understand the end-to-end latency and identify areas for optimization. In summary, choreography offers a decentralized approach to communication in microservices architectures, enabling services to interact autonomously without relying on a central orchestrator. Deploying choreography-based communication involves using message brokers or event-driven systems to facilitate message exchange between services, while resilience patterns and monitoring tools help manage the complexity and ensure the reliability of the system.CLI commands and container orchestration tools provide convenient ways to deploy and manage choreography-based communication, enabling developers and operators to build scalable, resilient, and maintainable microservices architectures effectively.

Orchestration plays a pivotal role in microservices architecture, offering centralized coordination to manage the interaction and execution of services within the system. Unlike the decentralized nature of choreography, where services communicate autonomously, orchestration involves a central orchestrator that coordinates the flow of communication and controls the execution of services. This centralized approach provides several advantages, including improved control, visibility, and manageability of the system as a whole. Deploying orchestration-based coordination in a microservices architecture often involves using container orchestration platforms such as Kubernetes or Docker Swarm. These platforms enable developers to define, deploy, and manage complex microservices-based applications using declarative configuration files. To deploy Kubernetes, for example, one can use the minikube start command to set up a local Kubernetes cluster for development and testing purposes. Similarly, the docker swarm init command initializes a Docker Swarm cluster, allowing services to be deployed and managed across multiple nodes. Once deployed, the orchestrator manages various aspects of the application lifecycle, including service discovery, load balancing, scaling, and fault tolerance. Kubernetes, for instance, uses concepts such as Pods, Services, Deployments, and StatefulSets to define and manage microservices within the cluster. YAML configuration files are used to specify the desired state of the application, with commands like kubectl apply -f <filename> used to apply these configurations to the Kubernetes cluster. Likewise, Docker Compose files can be used to define multi-container applications and services, with commands like docker-compose up -d used to deploy and manage the application using Docker Swarm. Orchestrators provide advanced features for managing the runtime environment of microservices, such as rolling updates, health checks, and auto-scaling. These features ensure the reliability and availability of services by automatically restarting failed instances, redistributing traffic during updates, and scaling resources based on demand. Additionally, orchestrators offer built-in support for service discovery and load balancing, enabling services to locate and communicate with each other dynamically. Kubernetes, for instance, provides a built-in DNS service that allows services to discover each other using DNS names. Similarly, Docker Swarm uses an overlay network to facilitate communication between services deployed across multiple nodes. Moreover, orchestrators offer robust security features to protect microservices and the underlying infrastructure from unauthorized access and attacks. These features include role-based access control (RBAC), network policies, and secure communication channels. By implementing these security measures, orchestrators help ensure the confidentiality, integrity, and availability of microservices and data within the system. CLI commands such as kubectl create role or docker stack deploy can be used to configure security policies and permissions within Kubernetes or Docker Swarm clusters. Monitoring and observability are essential aspects of managing orchestration-based microservices architectures. Tools such as Prometheus, Grafana, or ELK stack can be deployed using commands like helm install or kubectl apply -f to monitor the health, performance, and activity of microservices and orchestrators. By collecting and analyzing metrics and logs generated by the system, operators can gain insights into the behavior of the application and infrastructure, identify potential issues or bottlenecks, and take corrective actions as needed. In summary, orchestration provides centralized coordination for microservices architectures, enabling developers to manage the interaction and execution of services effectively. By deploying container orchestration platforms such as Kubernetes or Docker Swarm, organizations can achieve improved control, visibility, and manageability of their microservices-based applications. CLI commands and container orchestration tools provide convenient ways to deploy and manage orchestration-based microservices architectures, empowering developers and operators to build scalable, reliable, and maintainable systems effectively.

Chapter 6: Implementing Fault Tolerance and Circuit Breaker Patterns

The Circuit Breaker Pattern is a crucial component in modern software architecture, especially in distributed systems like microservices, where services depend on each other for functionality. It acts as a safeguard mechanism to prevent cascading failures and degradation of service performance caused by faulty or slow downstream services. The pattern borrows its name from its similarity to electrical circuit breakers, which halt the flow of electricity when a fault occurs to prevent damage to the system. In software, the Circuit Breaker Pattern operates similarly, monitoring requests to a service and "tripping" or "opening" the circuit when the service fails to respond within a specified threshold. This prevents further requests from being sent to the failing service until it has recovered, reducing the load on the system and allowing it to gracefully degrade instead of collapsing entirely. Implementing the Circuit Breaker Pattern typically involves three states: Closed, Open, and Half-Open. In the Closed state, the circuit breaker allows requests to pass through to the service as normal, monitoring their success or failure rates. When the failure rate exceeds a predefined threshold over a certain period, the circuit breaker transitions to the Open state, indicating that the service is unavailable or experiencing issues. In this state, the circuit breaker immediately rejects any requests to the service, preventing additional load and allowing it to recover. CLI commands such as **kubectl get pods** or **docker ps** can be used to monitor the status of services and identify when the Circuit Breaker Pattern should be activated. After a predefined cooldown period or when certain conditions are met, the circuit breaker transitions to the Half-Open state, allowing a limited number of requests to pass through to the service to test its availability. If these requests succeed, the circuit breaker transitions back to the Closed state, resuming normal operation. However, if the requests fail, the circuit breaker returns to the Open state, indicating that the service is still unavailable or unreliable. One popular implementation of the Circuit Breaker Pattern is provided by libraries like Netflix Hystrix or resilience4j in Java, which offer robust support for circuit breaking, fallbacks, and metrics collection. These libraries can be integrated into microservices using build tools like Maven or Gradle, with dependencies specified in the project's configuration files. For instance, adding the Hystrix dependency to a Maven project involves adding the following snippet to the project's **pom.xml** file:

xmlCopy code

```
<dependency>    <groupId>com.netflix.hystrix</groupId>
<artifactId>hystrix-core</artifactId>
<version>${hystrix.version}</version>  </dependency>
```

Similarly, resilience4j can be added as a dependency in a Gradle project by specifying the following in the **build.gradle** file:

groovyCopy code

```
implementation        'io.github.resilience4j:resilience4j-circuitbreaker'
```

Once integrated, developers can annotate methods or service calls with circuit breaker annotations to enable circuit breaking behavior. For example, in Spring Boot applications, the **@CircuitBreaker** annotation can be added to methods to enable circuit breaking for remote service calls. Additionally, metrics and monitoring tools such as Prometheus and Grafana can be used to monitor the health and performance of circuit breakers and downstream services. By collecting and analyzing metrics such as error rates, response times, and circuit breaker state transitions, operators can gain insights into the behavior of the system and identify potential issues or bottlenecks. Deploying Prometheus and Grafana involves using Helm charts or Kubernetes manifests to define and deploy the necessary resources to the cluster. Once deployed, metrics can be scraped from services and exposed to Prometheus using annotations or configuration settings. Grafana dashboards can then be configured to visualize these metrics and provide real-time insights into the health and performance of the system. In summary, the Circuit Breaker Pattern is a critical component in modern software architecture, providing resilience and fault tolerance in distributed systems. By implementing circuit breaking mechanisms using libraries like Netflix Hystrix or resilience4j, developers can protect their systems from cascading failures and ensure graceful degradation under adverse conditions. CLI commands and monitoring tools offer convenient ways to deploy and manage circuit breakers and monitor their performance in real-time, enabling operators to maintain the reliability and availability of their services effectively.

In the realm of microservices architecture, ensuring reliability and resilience is paramount, and one essential aspect of achieving this is implementing effective retrying strategies and fallback mechanisms. Retrying strategies and fallback mechanisms provide mechanisms for dealing with transient failures, network glitches, or unexpected errors that may occur during service-to-service communication. These strategies aim to improve the overall robustness of the system by allowing services to recover gracefully from failures and continue to operate even under adverse conditions. Deploying retrying strategies and fallback mechanisms typically involves integrating libraries or frameworks that provide support for these patterns into microservices applications. One popular library for implementing retrying strategies and fallback mechanisms is resilience4j, which offers comprehensive support for various resilience patterns, including retrying and fallback. Integrating resilience4j into microservices applications involves adding the necessary dependencies to the project's build configuration file, such as Maven's **pom.xml** or Gradle's **build.gradle** file. For example, to add resilience4j to a Maven project, developers can include the following dependency snippet in the **pom.xml** file:

xmlCopy code

```
<dependency>
<groupId>io.github.resilience4j</groupId>
<artifactId>resilience4j-retry</artifactId>
<version>1.7.0</version> </dependency>
```

Similarly, for Gradle projects, resilience4j can be added as a dependency in the **build.gradle** file using the following configuration:

groovyCopy code

```
implementation        'io.github.resilience4j:resilience4j-
retry:1.7.0'
```

Once integrated, developers can configure retrying strategies and fallback mechanisms using annotations or configuration settings provided by the resilience4j library. For example, the **@Retry** annotation can be added to methods or service calls to enable automatic retrying with customizable retry policies. Developers can specify parameters such as maximum number of retries, retry interval, and retry conditions to tailor the retry behavior to their specific requirements. Additionally, resilience4j provides support for fallback mechanisms, allowing developers to define fallback methods or behaviors that are invoked when a service call fails or exceeds the specified retry limit. This enables services to gracefully degrade or provide alternative functionality when the primary service is unavailable or experiencing issues. Monitoring and observability are essential aspects of managing retrying strategies and fallback mechanisms in microservices architectures. Tools such as Prometheus, Grafana, or ELK stack can be deployed using commands like **helm install** or **kubectl apply -f** to monitor the health, performance, and activity of microservices instances and resilience patterns. By collecting and analyzing metrics and logs generated by the system, operators can gain insights into the behavior of the application and identify potential issues or bottlenecks. For example, Prometheus can be configured to scrape metrics exposed by resilience4j and other monitoring tools, while Grafana can be used to visualize these metrics and create dashboards for real-time monitoring. Furthermore, distributed tracing tools like Jaeger or Zipkin can be deployed to trace the flow of requests through the system and identify areas for optimization or improvement. By instrumenting microservices with distributed tracing, developers can gain visibility into the latency and performance of service-to-service communication, helping to diagnose and troubleshoot issues more effectively. In summary, retrying strategies and fallback mechanisms are essential components of resilient microservices architectures, enabling services to recover gracefully from failures and continue to operate reliably under adverse conditions. By integrating libraries like resilience4j and deploying monitoring and observability tools, organizations can build robust and reliable microservices-based systems that can withstand transient failures and provide uninterrupted service to users. CLI commands and container orchestration tools offer convenient ways to deploy and manage resilience patterns and monitoring infrastructure, empowering developers and operators to build and maintain resilient microservices architectures effectively.

Chapter 7: Securing Microservices: Authentication and Authorization

OAuth2 and JSON Web Tokens (JWT) are fundamental components in modern authentication and authorization protocols, playing a crucial role in securing web applications and APIs. OAuth2, an open standard for access delegation, provides a framework for granting limited access to protected resources without sharing user credentials. It enables users to authorize third-party applications to access their data stored on a server, such as profiles, photos, or contacts, without revealing their credentials. Deploying OAuth2 typically involves configuring authorization servers and clients to support the OAuth2 protocol. One common open-source authorization server implementation is Keycloak, which can be deployed using Docker containers. To deploy Keycloak using Docker, developers can use the following command:

bashCopy code

```
docker run -d --name keycloak -p 8080:8080 jboss/keycloak
```

This command starts a Keycloak server instance running on port 8080, ready to handle OAuth2 authorization requests from clients. Once deployed, developers can configure clients and define authorization policies using Keycloak's administrative console. OAuth2 relies on the concept of access tokens, which are issued by the authorization server and used by clients to access protected resources on behalf of the user. These tokens can be either opaque or self-contained, with JWT being a popular choice for self-contained tokens due to their flexibility and ease of use. JSON Web Tokens (JWT) are encoded as compact URL-safe strings and contain claims that represent information about the user, such as their identity, roles, and permissions. Deploying JWT-based authentication involves generating and validating tokens using cryptographic algorithms such as HMAC or RSA. Libraries such as Nimbus JOSE + JWT for Java or jsonwebtoken for Node.js provide support for generating and parsing JWT tokens programmatically. For example, developers can use the jsonwebtoken library in Node.js to generate a JWT token with the following command:

bashCopy code

```
npm install jsonwebtoken
```

Once installed, developers can use the library to create JWT tokens with custom claims and sign them using a secret or private key. These tokens can then be included in HTTP requests as bearer tokens to authenticate users and authorize access to protected resources. When receiving a JWT token from a client, servers can validate the token's signature and claims to ensure its authenticity and integrity. Additionally, JWT tokens can be configured with expiration times and audience restrictions to mitigate security risks such as token replay attacks and token leakage. Integrating OAuth2 with JWT tokens provides a robust and secure authentication and authorization solution for web applications and APIs. OAuth2 handles the authorization flow, allowing clients to obtain access tokens from the authorization server, while JWT tokens serve as the means of authenticating users and authorizing access to protected resources. This combination of OAuth2 and JWT enables developers to implement secure, stateless authentication mechanisms that scale well and provide a seamless user experience. However, deploying OAuth2 and JWT-based authentication requires careful consideration of security best practices and implementation details. Developers must ensure that access tokens are securely transmitted and stored, that tokens are validated correctly, and that appropriate measures are in place to protect against common security threats such as token tampering and token replay attacks. Furthermore, monitoring and auditing mechanisms should be implemented to track token usage and detect suspicious activities. By following these best practices and leveraging OAuth2 and JWT effectively, developers can build secure and scalable web applications and APIs that protect user data and provide a seamless user experience. In summary, OAuth2 and JSON Web Tokens (JWT) are essential components in modern authentication and authorization protocols, providing secure and scalable solutions for protecting web applications and APIs. Deploying OAuth2 and JWT-based authentication involves configuring authorization servers and clients to support the OAuth2 protocol and generating and validating JWT tokens using cryptographic algorithms. By integrating OAuth2 with JWT, developers can implement robust and stateless authentication mechanisms that ensure the security and integrity of user data. CLI commands and libraries provide convenient ways to deploy and manage OAuth2 servers, clients, and JWT tokens, enabling developers to build secure and scalable authentication solutions effectively. Role-Based Access Control (RBAC) is a widely adopted authorization mechanism in microservices architecture, providing a flexible and scalable approach to managing access permissions within an application. RBAC allows administrators to define roles that represent sets of permissions, and assign these roles to users or groups based on their responsibilities or privileges. Deploying RBAC in microservices typically involves implementing RBAC logic within the application code and integrating it with authentication mechanisms to enforce access control policies. One common approach is to use middleware or filters to intercept incoming requests and verify the user's role and permissions before allowing access to protected resources. For example, in a Node.js application using Express.js, developers can use middleware functions to implement RBAC logic and enforce access control policies. The following code snippet demonstrates how middleware can be used to restrict access to a resource based on the user's role:

javascriptCopy code

```javascript
const express = require('express'); const app = express(); // Middleware to verify user's role const authorize = (req, res, next) => { // Check if user is authenticated and has the required role if (req.user && req.user.role === 'admin') { // User has the required role, proceed to the next middleware next(); }
```

```
else { // User does not have the required role, return
403 Forbidden res.status(403).send('Forbidden'); } };
// Protected route that requires admin role
app.get('/admin', authorize, (req, res) => { // Return
data for admin users res.send('Admin dashboard'); });
// Start the server app.listen(3000, () => {
console.log('Server is running on port 3000'); });
```

In this example, the **authorize** middleware checks if the user is authenticated and has the required role ('admin') before allowing access to the '/admin' route. If the user does not have the required role, the middleware returns a 403 Forbidden response, denying access to the resource. Deploying RBAC also involves defining roles and permissions within the application, typically through configuration files or databases. For example, developers can define roles and their associated permissions in a JSON or YAML file, which is then loaded by the application during startup. This allows administrators to easily manage roles and permissions without modifying the application code. Once roles and permissions are defined, developers can use them to enforce access control policies throughout the application. For instance, they can check the user's role and permissions before allowing them to perform certain actions or access specific resources. RBAC can also be integrated with external identity providers and access management systems to centralize user authentication and authorization. For example, organizations can use OAuth2 providers like Keycloak or Okta to authenticate users and obtain their roles and permissions, which are then used by microservices to enforce access control policies. Integrating RBAC with external identity providers typically involves configuring the provider to issue JSON Web Tokens (JWT) containing user roles and permissions, which are then validated by microservices during request processing. CLI commands such as **kubectl apply -f** or **docker run** are often used to deploy RBAC policies and configurations to Kubernetes clusters or Docker containers. For example, organizations can use Kubernetes Role-Based Access Control (RBAC) to define roles and permissions for accessing cluster resources. They can create Role and RoleBinding objects using YAML configuration files and apply them to the cluster using the **kubectl apply -f** command. Similarly, organizations can use Docker Compose or Kubernetes manifests to define RBAC policies and configurations for containerized microservices applications and deploy them using Docker or Kubernetes. Monitoring and auditing RBAC policies and access control decisions are essential aspects of managing RBAC in microservices architecture. Tools such as Prometheus, Grafana, or ELK stack can be deployed to monitor RBAC-related metrics and logs and detect anomalous behavior or security incidents. By collecting and analyzing RBAC-related data, organizations can gain insights into access patterns, identify potential security risks, and ensure compliance with regulatory requirements. In summary, Role-Based Access Control (RBAC) is a vital component of microservices architecture, providing a flexible and scalable approach to managing access permissions within an application. Deploying RBAC involves implementing RBAC logic within the application code, defining roles and permissions, integrating with authentication mechanisms, and monitoring access control decisions. CLI commands and configuration tools facilitate the deployment and management of RBAC policies and configurations, enabling organizations to build secure and compliant microservices architectures effectively.

Chapter 8: Continuous Integration and Continuous Deployment (CI/CD) Pipelines

Continuous Integration/Continuous Deployment (CI/CD) has become a cornerstone in modern software development, particularly in the context of microservices architecture. CI/CD pipelines automate the process of building, testing, and deploying software changes, enabling teams to deliver updates to production environments rapidly and reliably. Implementing CI/CD best practices is crucial for maximizing the efficiency, quality, and stability of microservices-based applications. Setting up a CI/CD pipeline typically involves configuring a set of tools and defining workflows that automate various stages of the software delivery process. Popular CI/CD platforms such as Jenkins, GitLab CI/CD, or CircleCI provide robust features for orchestrating CI/CD pipelines and integrating them with version control systems like Git. Developers can use CLI commands to set up Jenkins, a widely used CI/CD tool, on a server or Kubernetes cluster. For example, to deploy Jenkins using Docker, developers can run the following command:

```
bashCopy code
docker run -d -p 8080:8080 -v jenkins_home:/var/jenkins_home jenkins/jenkins:lts
```

This command starts a Jenkins server instance running on port 8080, with persistent storage mounted to the local file system. Once Jenkins is up and running, developers can create pipelines using Jenkinsfile, a text-based script that defines the steps of the CI/CD process. Jenkinsfile allows developers to specify stages such as building, testing, and deploying, along with their respective commands and dependencies. Similarly, GitLab CI/CD provides a declarative configuration syntax called .gitlab-ci.yml, which allows developers to define CI/CD pipelines directly within their GitLab repositories. By committing .gitlab-ci.yml to the repository, developers can trigger automated builds and deployments whenever changes are pushed to the repository. One of the key principles of CI/CD best practices is to automate as much of the software delivery process as possible. This includes automating tests at various levels, such as unit tests, integration tests, and end-to-end tests, to ensure the quality and correctness of software changes. For example, developers can use testing frameworks like JUnit, Mockito, or Jest to write unit tests for individual components or services and integrate them into the CI/CD pipeline. Integration tests can be automated using tools like Postman, Newman, or RestAssured to verify the behavior of APIs and services in a real-world environment. End-to-end tests, which simulate user interactions with the application, can be automated using frameworks like Selenium or Cypress. Another best practice in CI/CD is to adopt a "fail fast" approach, where errors and failures are detected early in the development process, allowing teams to address them before they propagate to production. This involves running tests and static code analysis tools as part of the CI/CD pipeline to identify issues such as bugs, security vulnerabilities, or performance bottlenecks. Static code analysis tools like SonarQube, ESLint, or Checkstyle can be integrated into CI/CD pipelines to automatically analyze code quality and enforce coding standards. By catching and fixing issues early in the development process, teams can reduce the risk of introducing defects and ensure that only high-quality code is deployed to production. Continuous deployment, the practice of automatically deploying changes to production environments after passing through the CI/CD pipeline, is another key aspect of CI/CD best practices. However, it's essential to implement safeguards such as automated tests, code reviews, and deployment gates to minimize the risk of deploying faulty or unstable changes. Techniques such as blue-green deployments, canary releases, or feature flags can also be employed to gradually roll out changes to production and mitigate the impact of potential failures. Blue-green deployments involve maintaining two identical production environments (blue and green) and switching traffic between them during deployments. Canary releases involve gradually exposing new features or changes to a subset of users before rolling them out to the entire user base. Feature flags allow developers to toggle features on or off at runtime, enabling them to control the exposure of new functionality and gather feedback from users. Monitoring and observability are essential components of CI/CD pipelines, providing visibility into the health, performance, and availability of applications and infrastructure. Tools such as Prometheus, Grafana, or

ELK stack can be integrated into CI/CD pipelines to collect and analyze metrics, logs, and traces generated by applications and services. By monitoring key performance indicators (KPIs) such as response time, error rate, and resource utilization, teams can identify issues, diagnose problems, and optimize the performance of their applications. Furthermore, CI/CD pipelines can be augmented with automated rollback mechanisms to quickly revert changes in case of deployment failures or degraded performance. By integrating monitoring and automated rollback into CI/CD pipelines, teams can ensure the reliability and resilience of their applications and respond quickly to incidents. In summary, CI/CD best practices are essential for optimizing the software delivery process in microservices architecture, enabling teams to deliver updates rapidly, reliably, and with high quality. By automating tests, adopting a fail-fast approach, implementing continuous deployment, and integrating monitoring and observability, teams can streamline their development workflows, reduce the risk of deploying faulty changes, and improve the overall efficiency and stability of their applications. CLI commands and configuration tools provide convenient ways to set up and manage CI/CD pipelines, empowering teams to embrace CI/CD best practices and accelerate their software delivery lifecycle.

Automated testing is a critical component of Continuous Integration/Continuous Deployment (CI/CD) pipelines in microservices architecture, ensuring that changes to codebases do not introduce regressions or bugs into the software. The practice of automated testing involves writing scripts or programs to execute tests automatically, validating the behavior and functionality of microservices throughout the development lifecycle. Implementing automated testing in CI/CD pipelines typically begins with defining test suites that cover different aspects of microservices functionality, including unit tests, integration tests, and end-to-end tests. Unit tests focus on testing individual components or functions in isolation, ensuring that each unit behaves as expected. Integration tests verify the interaction between different microservices or modules, validating the integration points and communication protocols. End-to-end tests, also known as functional tests, simulate real user scenarios and validate the behavior of the entire system from end to end. Each type of test plays a crucial role in ensuring the quality and reliability of microservices applications. To execute automated tests in CI/CD pipelines, developers leverage testing frameworks and tools suitable for the programming languages and technologies used in their microservices ecosystem. For example, popular testing frameworks like JUnit, Mockito, and TestNG are commonly used for Java-based microservices, while Mocha, Chai, and Jest are popular choices for Node.js applications. These frameworks provide utilities for writing and executing tests, asserting expected behaviors, and generating test reports. Integration with CI/CD pipelines involves configuring build scripts or pipeline definitions to trigger automated tests automatically whenever code changes are pushed to version control repositories. For instance, in a Jenkins CI/CD pipeline, developers can use the Jenkinsfile to define stages and steps for building, testing, and deploying microservices. The following snippet demonstrates how to define a testing stage in a Jenkins pipeline:

groovyCopy code

```
pipeline { agent any stages { stage('Build') { steps { // Build microservices artifacts sh 'mvn clean package' } } stage('Test') { steps { // Run automated tests sh 'mvn test' } } stage('Deploy') { steps { // Deploy microservices to Kubernetes cluster sh 'kubectl apply -f deployment.yaml' } } } }
```

In this example, the 'Test' stage executes automated tests using the 'mvn test' command, which triggers the execution of unit tests and integration tests defined in the Maven project. Similarly, for Node.js applications, developers can use npm scripts or custom shell commands to execute tests as part of the CI/CD pipeline. For instance, the following npm script runs Mocha tests for a Node.js application:

jsonCopy code

```
"scripts": { "test": "mocha test/**/*.spec.js" }
```

Once automated tests are executed, CI/CD pipelines generate test reports and artifacts, providing insights into test coverage, test results, and potential issues or failures. Test reports can be published to CI/CD platforms such as Jenkins, CircleCI, or GitLab CI/CD, allowing developers and stakeholders to review test results and make informed decisions about the quality of microservices releases. Additionally, automated testing enables developers to implement Continuous Testing practices, where tests are run continuously throughout the development lifecycle, providing fast feedback on code changes and ensuring that only high-quality code is promoted to production environments. Continuous Testing reduces the risk of introducing bugs and regressions into microservices applications, improving software reliability and user satisfaction. To further enhance automated testing in CI/CD pipelines, developers can leverage techniques such as parallel test execution, test data management, and test environment orchestration. Parallel test execution involves running tests concurrently across multiple environments or nodes, reducing test execution time and improving pipeline throughput. Test data management focuses on ensuring that test data is consistent, relevant, and up-to-date, enabling reliable and repeatable test executions. Test environment orchestration involves automating the provisioning and configuration of test environments, ensuring that tests are executed in environments that closely resemble production settings. CLI commands such as **docker-compose up** or **kubectl apply -f** are often used to deploy test environments and dependencies required for running automated tests. For example, developers can use Docker Compose to define and deploy containers for databases, message brokers, or external services used in integration tests. Similarly, Kubernetes manifests can be applied to provision test environments in Kubernetes clusters, ensuring consistency between development, testing, and production environments. In summary, automated testing is a fundamental practice in CI/CD pipelines for microservices, enabling developers to validate the functionality and behavior of microservices applications efficiently. By leveraging testing frameworks, CI/CD platforms, and infrastructure automation tools, developers can implement automated testing practices that ensure the reliability, scalability, and maintainability of microservices deployments. Continuous Testing practices, parallel test execution, and test environment orchestration further enhance the effectiveness and efficiency of automated testing, enabling organizations to deliver high-quality software continuously and reliably.

Chapter 9: Monitoring and Observability in Microservices

Metrics, logs, and tracing are essential components of observability in microservices architecture, providing insights into the performance, behavior, and health of distributed systems. Deploying and managing metrics, logs, and tracing infrastructure involves setting up monitoring agents, configuring data collection, and integrating with observability platforms. Metrics are quantitative measurements that track various aspects of microservices performance, such as resource utilization, throughput, and error rates. Logs, on the other hand, capture textual data about system events, errors, and user interactions, providing a detailed record of application activity. Tracing complements metrics and logs by providing end-to-end visibility into distributed transactions and requests, enabling developers to identify performance bottlenecks and troubleshoot issues across microservices boundaries. To deploy metrics, logs, and tracing in microservices architecture, developers often use open-source monitoring solutions such as Prometheus, Grafana, and Jaeger, which offer comprehensive features for collecting, visualizing, and analyzing observability data. These tools can be deployed using container orchestration platforms like Kubernetes or Docker Compose, allowing developers to scale monitoring infrastructure alongside microservices deployments. For example, deploying Prometheus and Grafana in a Kubernetes cluster involves defining manifests for Prometheus server and Grafana deployment, and then applying them using **kubectl apply -f**. The following commands demonstrate how to deploy Prometheus and Grafana using Kubernetes manifests:

```bash
bashCopy code
kubectl apply -f https://raw.githubusercontent.com/prometheus-operator/kube-prometheus/main/manifests/setup.yaml kubectl apply -f https://raw.githubusercontent.com/prometheus-operator/kube-prometheus/main/manifests/ kubectl apply -f https://raw.githubusercontent.com/prometheus-operator/kube-prometheus/main/manifests/grafana-dashboardDefinition.yaml
```

These commands deploy Prometheus Operator and its related custom resources, including Prometheus server, Alertmanager, and Grafana. Once deployed, Prometheus starts collecting metrics from microservices and infrastructure components, while Grafana provides a graphical interface for visualizing and analyzing metrics data. In addition to metrics collection, logging is essential for troubleshooting issues and auditing system activity in microservices architecture. Popular logging solutions like Elasticsearch, Fluentd, and Kibana (EFK stack) or Loki and Fluent Bit are commonly used to aggregate, parse, and store logs generated by microservices. Deploying logging infrastructure involves deploying logging agents or sidecars alongside microservices containers to collect and forward logs to centralized logging systems. For example, deploying Fluentd and Elasticsearch in a Kubernetes cluster involves defining manifests for Fluentd DaemonSet and Elasticsearch StatefulSet, and then applying them using **kubectl apply -f**. The following commands demonstrate how to deploy Fluentd and Elasticsearch using Kubernetes manifests:

bashCopy code

```
kubectl                apply               -f
https://raw.githubusercontent.com/fluent/fluentd-
kubernetes-daemonset/master/fluentd-daemonset-
elasticsearch.yaml       kubectl       apply      -f
https://download.elastic.co/downloads/eck/2.3.0/all-
in-one.yaml
```

These commands deploy Fluentd as a DaemonSet in the Kubernetes cluster, ensuring that each node collects and forwards logs to Elasticsearch. Elasticsearch, deployed using the Elastic Cloud on Kubernetes (ECK) operator, provides a scalable and resilient storage backend for storing and indexing logs. Tracing infrastructure, such as Jaeger, Zipkin, or OpenTelemetry, enables developers to trace requests and monitor latency across microservices interactions. Deploying tracing infrastructure involves deploying tracing agents or sidecars alongside microservices containers to capture and propagate trace spans. For example, deploying Jaeger in a Kubernetes cluster involves defining manifests for Jaeger Agent and Jaeger Collector, and then applying them using **kubectl apply -**

f. The following commands demonstrate how to deploy Jaeger using Kubernetes manifests:

```
bashCopy code
kubectl create namespace observability kubectl apply -f
https://raw.githubusercontent.com/jaegertracing/jaeg
er-kubernetes/master/all-in-one/jaeger-all-in-one-
template.yml -n observability
```

These commands create a namespace for observability resources and deploy Jaeger components, including the Jaeger Agent, Collector, Query, and Ingester, in the Kubernetes cluster. Once deployed, Jaeger starts capturing traces from microservices and provides a web-based interface for visualizing and analyzing distributed traces. In summary, deploying metrics, logs, and tracing infrastructure is essential for gaining visibility into microservices architecture, enabling developers to monitor and troubleshoot applications effectively. By leveraging open-source monitoring solutions and container orchestration platforms, developers can deploy scalable and resilient observability infrastructure alongside microservices deployments, ensuring reliability and performance in distributed systems.

Distributed tracing is a critical technique in microservices architecture for understanding and debugging complex interactions between services. It allows developers to trace the flow of requests as they propagate through various microservices, providing insights into performance bottlenecks, latency issues, and errors. OpenTelemetry is an open-source project that provides a set of APIs, libraries, and tools for collecting distributed traces and telemetry data from applications and services. It aims to standardize the instrumentation, collection, and export of telemetry data across different programming languages and frameworks, making it easier to monitor and debug microservices applications. Deploying OpenTelemetry involves instrumenting microservices code to generate trace data and configuring exporters to send this data to backend systems for storage, analysis, and visualization. One common backend system used with OpenTelemetry is Jaeger, an open-source distributed tracing platform that provides visualization and analysis of trace data. To deploy Jaeger, developers can use Docker to run Jaeger components as Docker containers. The following command starts a Jaeger all-in-one Docker container:

bashCopy code

```
docker run -d --name jaeger \ -e COLLECTOR_ZIPKIN_HTTP_PORT=9411 \ -p 16686:16686 -p 9411:9411 \ jaegertracing/all-in-one:latest
```

This command starts a Jaeger all-in-one container with the Jaeger UI available on port 16686 and the Zipkin-compatible HTTP endpoint available on port 9411. Once Jaeger is running, developers can instrument their microservices code to generate trace data using OpenTelemetry libraries. For example, in a Node.js application, developers can use the **@opentelemetry/node** package to instrument their code and generate traces. The following code snippet demonstrates how to create an OpenTelemetry tracer and use it to generate traces in a Node.js application: javascriptCopy code

```
const { NodeTracerProvider } = require('@opentelemetry/node'); const { SimpleSpanProcessor } = require('@opentelemetry/tracing'); const { JaegerExporter } = require('@opentelemetry/exporter-jaeger'); const provider = new NodeTracerProvider(); const exporter = new JaegerExporter({ serviceName: 'my-service', host: 'localhost', port: 6832, }); provider.addSpanProcessor(new SimpleSpanProcessor(exporter)); provider.register();
```

In this example, the code creates a new tracer provider using the **@opentelemetry/node** package and configures it to export trace data to a Jaeger backend running on localhost. Developers can then instrument their code by creating spans to represent individual operations or requests and adding them to the trace. Spans can include metadata such as operation names, tags, and logs, providing detailed information about the execution of microservices. Once the code is instrumented, developers can run their microservices and generate trace data, which is then sent to the Jaeger backend for storage and analysis. In addition to Jaeger, OpenTelemetry supports other backend systems and exporters, including Zipkin, Prometheus, and AWS X-Ray, allowing developers to choose the most suitable backend for their monitoring and tracing needs.

Deploying and configuring OpenTelemetry with different backend systems may require additional setup and configuration, depending on the chosen backend. However, OpenTelemetry provides comprehensive documentation and examples to help developers get started with instrumentation and tracing. Once traces are collected and stored in the backend, developers can use visualization tools provided by the backend system to analyze and debug trace data. These tools allow developers to explore individual traces, view service dependencies, identify performance bottlenecks, and troubleshoot errors in microservices applications. Tracing data can also be integrated with logging and metrics systems to provide a holistic view of microservices performance and behavior. Overall, Distributed Tracing with OpenTelemetry is a powerful technique for monitoring and debugging microservices applications, providing developers with insights into request flows, performance metrics, and error conditions. By instrumenting microservices code with OpenTelemetry libraries and configuring exporters to send trace data to backend systems, developers can gain visibility into the behavior of their applications and improve reliability, performance, and scalability.

Chapter 10: Best Practices for Documentation and Collaboration in Microservices Development

API documentation plays a pivotal role in modern software development, enabling developers to understand, consume, and integrate with APIs effectively. Swagger, now known as the OpenAPI Specification, is a widely adopted standard for describing RESTful APIs. It provides a machine-readable format for documenting APIs, making it easier to generate client libraries, perform automated testing, and foster collaboration between teams. The OpenAPI Specification defines a structured way to describe API endpoints, request/response payloads, authentication methods, and error handling. Deploying OpenAPI Specification involves creating a YAML or JSON file that adheres to the specification guidelines. To create an OpenAPI Specification document, developers can use tools like Swagger Editor, an online editor that provides a user-friendly interface for writing and validating OpenAPI documents. Alternatively, developers can use CLI commands to install Swagger Editor locally and edit OpenAPI files offline. The following command installs Swagger Editor using npm:

bashCopy code

```
npm install -g swagger-editor
```

Once installed, developers can launch Swagger Editor using the following command:

bashCopy code

```
swagger-editor
```

This command opens a web browser with Swagger Editor running locally, allowing developers to create and edit

OpenAPI Specification documents. Within Swagger Editor, developers can define API paths, parameters, request/response schemas, and other metadata using YAML or JSON syntax. For example, the following snippet demonstrates a basic OpenAPI Specification document describing a simple RESTful API:

yamlCopy code

```
openapi: 3.0.0 info: title: Sample API version: 1.0.0
paths: /users: get: summary: Retrieve a list of users
responses: '200': description: OK content:
application/json: schema: type: array items: type:
object properties: id: type: integer name: type: string
```

In this example, the OpenAPI Specification document defines a single endpoint (**/users**) with a **GET** operation to retrieve a list of users. The **responses** section specifies the expected response format, including a **200 OK** response with a JSON array containing user objects. Along with defining API endpoints and operations, the OpenAPI Specification allows developers to document request parameters, query parameters, request bodies, headers, and authentication mechanisms. By adhering to the OpenAPI Specification, developers ensure consistency and clarity in API documentation, making it easier for consumers to understand and interact with APIs. Once an OpenAPI Specification document is created, developers can use it to generate interactive API documentation using tools like Swagger UI. Swagger UI is a web-based tool that renders OpenAPI Specification documents as interactive API documentation, allowing users to explore endpoints, make requests, and view responses in real-time. To deploy Swagger UI, developers can use Docker to run Swagger UI as a Docker container. The following command starts a

Swagger UI container that serves API documentation on port 8080:

bashCopy code

```
docker run -d --name swagger-ui -p 8080:8080 swaggerapi/swagger-ui
```

Once the container is running, developers can access the Swagger UI interface by navigating to **http://localhost:8080** in a web browser. Swagger UI will automatically load the OpenAPI Specification document hosted at the specified URL, providing an interactive documentation experience for consumers. In addition to Swagger UI, developers can use other tools and libraries to generate client SDKs, server stubs, and automated tests from OpenAPI Specification documents. These tools automate the process of consuming and integrating with APIs, reducing development time and improving the overall developer experience. Overall, API documentation with Swagger, now known as the OpenAPI Specification, is essential for building and consuming RESTful APIs in modern software development. By creating structured, machine-readable documentation that adheres to the OpenAPI Specification, developers can foster collaboration, streamline integration, and enhance the usability of their APIs for consumers.

Collaborative development tools have revolutionized the way software is built, enabling teams to collaborate seamlessly on projects regardless of geographical location. At the heart of modern collaborative development workflows is Git, a distributed version control system designed for managing codebases efficiently. Git allows developers to track changes to source code, collaborate with team members, and manage project history effectively. Deploying Git involves installing Git on a local machine and configuring it to interact with remote repositories hosted on platforms like GitLab or GitHub. To install Git on a Linux-based system using apt package manager, developers can use the following command:

bashCopy code

```
sudo apt-get update sudo apt-get install git
```

Once Git is installed, developers can configure their identity using the following commands:

bashCopy code

```
git config --global user.name "Your Name" git config --global user.email "your.email@example.com"
```

These commands set the global user name and email address associated with Git commits. With Git configured, developers can clone remote repositories to their local machines using the **git clone** command. For example, to clone a repository from GitHub, developers can use the following command:

bashCopy code

```
git clone https://github.com/user/repo.git
```

This command clones the repository from the specified URL to the local machine, creating a copy of the repository's codebase. Once the repository is cloned, developers can make changes to the codebase, stage their changes using the **git add** command, and commit them using the **git commit** command. For example, the following commands stage all changes and commit them with a descriptive message:

bashCopy code

```
git add . git commit -m "Add new feature"
```

After committing changes, developers can push their commits to the remote repository using the **git push** command. For example, to push commits to the **master** branch of a GitHub repository, developers can use the following command:

bashCopy code

```
git push origin master
```

This command pushes local commits to the **master** branch of the remote repository hosted on GitHub. In addition to basic version control functionality, Git also provides powerful branching and merging capabilities, allowing developers to work on features and bug fixes in isolated branches before merging them back into the main codebase. Collaborative development platforms like GitLab and GitHub build on top of Git's core functionality, providing additional features and tools for managing projects, tracking issues, and facilitating code reviews. GitLab is an open-source platform for DevOps lifecycle management, offering features such as integrated CI/CD pipelines, issue tracking, and wiki pages. To deploy GitLab, developers can use Docker to run GitLab as a Docker container. The following command starts a GitLab container using the official GitLab Docker image:

bashCopy code

```
docker run --detach \ --hostname gitlab.example.com \ --publish 443:443 --publish 80:80 --publish 22:22 \ --name gitlab \ --restart always \ --volume /srv/gitlab/config:/etc/gitlab \ --volume /srv/gitlab/logs:/var/log/gitlab \ --volume /srv/gitlab/data:/var/opt/gitlab \ gitlab/gitlab-ce:latest
```

This command starts a GitLab container with HTTPS enabled, exposing ports 443, 80, and 22 for web, Git, and SSH access respectively. GitHub, on the other hand, is a web-based platform for hosting Git repositories and collaborating on projects. It offers features such as pull requests, code reviews, and project management tools. To deploy GitHub, developers can create an account on the GitHub website and create repositories to host their projects. GitHub provides a web interface for managing repositories, creating issues, and reviewing code changes, making it easy for teams to collaborate on software projects. In addition to hosting code, GitHub also integrates with various third-party services and tools, including CI/CD platforms, code quality analysis tools, and project management systems. Overall, collaborative development tools like Git, GitLab, and GitHub have transformed the way software is developed, enabling teams to work together efficiently, iterate on codebases rapidly, and deliver high-quality software products. By leveraging these tools, developers can streamline collaboration, improve productivity, and build better software faster.

BOOK 3
MASTERING MICROSERVICES
ADVANCED TECHNIQUES FOR OPTIMIZING
PERFORMANCE AND SECURITY

ROB BOTWRIGHT

Chapter 1: Advanced Load Balancing Strategies for Microservices

Dynamic load balancing is a crucial aspect of modern distributed systems, ensuring optimal resource utilization and high availability under varying traffic conditions. Load balancers distribute incoming traffic across multiple backend servers, preventing overloading of individual servers and improving overall system performance. There are several dynamic load balancing techniques employed in distributed systems, each with its own advantages and use cases. One such technique is Round Robin, a simple yet effective method where incoming requests are sequentially distributed across a pool of backend servers in a circular manner. Deploying Round Robin load balancing can be achieved using various load balancing solutions such as Nginx or HAProxy. For example, to configure Nginx for Round Robin load balancing, developers can edit the Nginx configuration file and define upstream servers as follows:

```
bashCopy code
upstream backend { server backend1.example.com;
server backend2.example.com; server
backend3.example.com; } server { listen 80;
server_name example.com; location / { proxy_pass
http://backend; } }
```

This configuration defines an upstream block with multiple backend servers and directs incoming traffic to them using the **proxy_pass** directive. Nginx will then distribute requests to these servers in a Round Robin fashion. Another dynamic load balancing technique is Least Connections, which directs incoming requests to the backend server with the fewest active connections at the time of the request. This technique is particularly useful for optimizing resource utilization and minimizing response times in scenarios where backend servers have varying loads. Implementing Least Connections load balancing can also be achieved using Nginx or HAProxy. To configure Nginx for Least Connections load balancing, developers can use the **least_conn** parameter within the upstream block:

bashCopy code

```
upstream backend { least_conn; server backend1.example.com; server backend2.example.com; server backend3.example.com; }
```

By specifying **least_conn**, Nginx will dynamically distribute incoming requests to the backend server with the fewest active connections, ensuring a balanced load distribution. Weighted Round Robin is another dynamic load balancing technique that assigns different weights to backend servers based on their capacity or performance characteristics. Servers with higher weights receive more traffic than servers with lower weights, allowing for fine-grained control over load distribution. Configuring Weighted Round Robin load balancing can also be achieved using Nginx or HAProxy by specifying weights for each server in the upstream block:

bashCopy code

```
upstream backend { server backend1.example.com weight=3; server backend2.example.com weight=2; server backend3.example.com weight=1; }
```

In this configuration, **backend1.example.com** will receive three times as much traffic as **backend3.example.com** due to its higher weight. Additionally, Dynamic Load Balancing Techniques include advanced algorithms such as Least Response Time, which directs requests to the backend server with the lowest response time, and IP Hashing, which uses a hash function to map client IP addresses to backend servers, ensuring that requests from the same client are always directed to the same server. These techniques are particularly useful for optimizing performance, ensuring session persistence, and enhancing user experience in distributed systems. Deploying these advanced load balancing techniques often requires specialized load balancing solutions or dedicated hardware appliances capable of implementing complex algorithms efficiently. Overall, Dynamic Load Balancing Techniques play a critical role in ensuring the scalability, reliability, and performance of modern distributed systems, enabling organizations to handle increasing traffic volumes and deliver seamless user experiences. By understanding the principles and implementations of these techniques, developers can design robust and efficient load balancing solutions tailored to their specific requirements. Load balancing across multiple regions is a critical strategy for ensuring high availability, fault tolerance, and optimal performance in distributed systems with a global user base. By distributing incoming traffic across geographically dispersed data centers or cloud regions, organizations can minimize latency, mitigate the impact of regional outages, and provide a consistent user experience worldwide. Deploying load balancing across multiple regions involves configuring a global load balancer that intelligently routes requests to the nearest or least congested data center based on factors such as network latency, server health, and geographic proximity. One widely used approach for achieving global load balancing is through the use of a Content Delivery Network (CDN), which caches content at edge locations worldwide and automatically routes user requests to the nearest edge server. CDNs such as Cloudflare, Amazon CloudFront, and Google Cloud CDN provide global load balancing capabilities out of the box, allowing organizations to distribute static and dynamic content efficiently across multiple regions. Configuring a global load balancer with Cloudflare, for example, involves signing up for a Cloudflare account, adding domains to the Cloudflare dashboard, and configuring DNS settings to point to Cloudflare's nameservers. Once configured, Cloudflare automatically routes user traffic to the nearest edge server, reducing latency and improving website performance. Another approach to load balancing across multiple regions is through the use of DNS-based load balancing solutions, such as Amazon Route 53 or Google Cloud DNS. These services allow organizations to create DNS records with multiple IP addresses corresponding to different data centers or cloud regions and automatically route traffic based on geographical location or health checks. Configuring DNS-based load balancing with Amazon Route 53 involves creating a new DNS record set, selecting the "Geoproximity" routing policy, and defining endpoint weights and health checks for each region. This allows Route 53 to intelligently route traffic to the closest healthy endpoint, ensuring optimal performance and availability for users worldwide. Additionally, organizations can deploy their own global load balancing solutions using software-defined networking (SDN) technologies such as Anycast or Multi-CDN. Anycast allows organizations to advertise the same IP address from multiple locations worldwide and automatically routes traffic to the nearest or least congested server based on network topology. Deploying Anycast involves configuring BGP routing protocols and announcing IP prefixes from multiple data centers or cloud regions. This allows organizations to achieve global load balancing without relying on third-party CDN providers. Similarly, Multi-CDN solutions leverage multiple CDN providers to distribute content across diverse networks and mitigate the risk of single points of failure. Deploying Multi-CDN involves integrating multiple CDN providers into the organization's infrastructure, configuring DNS records to route traffic to the most performant CDN based on real-time metrics, and implementing failover mechanisms to handle CDN outages or performance degradation. In addition to improving performance and availability, load balancing across multiple regions also helps organizations comply with data sovereignty regulations by ensuring that user data remains within the jurisdiction of the user's country or region. By distributing workloads across multiple regions, organizations can also scale resources dynamically in response to changing demand and traffic patterns, reducing costs and improving resource utilization. Overall, load balancing across multiple regions is a crucial component of modern distributed systems architecture, enabling organizations to deliver fast, reliable, and scalable services to users worldwide. Whether leveraging CDNs, DNS-based solutions, or custom SDN technologies, organizations must carefully design and implement global load balancing strategies to meet the unique requirements of their applications and user base.

Chapter 2: Optimizing Microservices Communication Protocols

Protocol Buffers (protobuf) and JSON are two popular data interchange formats used in modern software development for serializing and deserializing structured data. While both formats serve similar purposes, they have distinct differences in terms of performance, efficiency, and ease of use. Protocol Buffers, developed by Google, is a binary serialization format that offers significant performance advantages over JSON due to its compact binary representation and efficient encoding scheme. To utilize Protocol Buffers, developers need to define a message schema using the Protocol Buffer Language (proto), compile it using the protocol buffer compiler (protoc), and generate language-specific code to serialize and deserialize messages. The protocol buffer compiler can be installed using package managers such as apt or Homebrew, depending on the operating system. For example, to install the protocol buffer compiler on Ubuntu, developers can use the following command:

bashCopy code

```
sudo apt-get install protobuf-compiler
```

Once installed, developers can define a message schema in a .proto file using the protocol buffer syntax, specifying message fields and their data types. For example, a simple .proto file defining a message with two fields, "id" and "name," might look like this:

protobufCopy code

```
syntax = "proto3"; message Person { int32 id = 1; string
name = 2; }
```
After defining the message schema, developers can compile it using the protocol buffer compiler to generate language-specific code for serialization and deserialization. For example, to compile the .proto file and generate Python code, developers can use the following command:

bashCopy code

```
protoc --python_out=. person.proto
```
This command generates a Python module (person_pb2.py) containing classes and methods for working with protocol buffer messages. Developers can then use these generated classes to serialize and deserialize messages in their Python applications. JSON, on the other hand, is a text-based data interchange format that is widely supported and easy to read and write by both humans and machines. Unlike Protocol Buffers, JSON does not require a schema definition, making it more flexible and easier to use in dynamic environments. However, JSON's text-based representation can result in larger message sizes compared to Protocol Buffers, leading to increased network bandwidth usage and slower serialization and deserialization performance. To serialize and deserialize JSON data in Python, developers can use the built-in json module, which provides functions for encoding Python objects to JSON strings and decoding JSON strings to Python objects. For example, to serialize a Python dictionary to a JSON string, developers can use the json.dumps() function:

```python
pythonCopy code
import json data = {'id': 1, 'name': 'John Doe'}
json_string = json.dumps(data)
```

This will produce a JSON string representing the dictionary {'id': 1, 'name': 'John Doe'}. Similarly, to deserialize a JSON string to a Python dictionary, developers can use the json.loads() function:

```python
pythonCopy code
json_string = '{"id": 1, "name": "John Doe"}' data = json.loads(json_string)
```

This will parse the JSON string and return a Python dictionary representing the data. When comparing the performance of Protocol Buffers and JSON, Protocol Buffers typically outperform JSON in terms of serialization and deserialization speed, message size, and network bandwidth usage. This is because Protocol Buffers use a binary encoding format that is more compact and efficient than JSON's text-based format, resulting in smaller message sizes and faster data transfer over the network. Additionally, Protocol Buffers' schema-based approach allows for faster serialization and deserialization compared to JSON's dynamic parsing of text-based data. However, JSON's human-readable format and lack of schema make it more suitable for scenarios where readability and flexibility are more important than performance, such as web APIs and configuration files. In contrast, Protocol Buffers are better suited for high-performance, resource-constrained environments where efficiency and scalability are paramount, such as microservices communication and interprocess communication. Overall, the choice between Protocol Buffers and JSON depends on the specific requirements and constraints of the application, including performance, readability, flexibility, and interoperability with existing systems. By understanding the strengths and weaknesses of each format, developers can make informed decisions when designing data interchange mechanisms for their applications.

Selecting the appropriate communication protocol is a crucial decision in software development, as it directly impacts the efficiency, performance, and scalability of distributed systems. Several factors must be considered when choosing a communication protocol, including the nature of the application, the requirements for data exchange, the network environment, and the constraints of the target platform. One of the most common communication protocols used in distributed systems is HTTP (Hypertext Transfer Protocol), a stateless protocol that facilitates communication between clients and servers over the internet. HTTP is widely supported, simple to implement, and suitable for a wide range of use cases, including web applications, APIs, and microservices architectures. Deploying an HTTP-based communication protocol involves setting up web servers and clients capable of sending and receiving HTTP requests and responses. For example, to deploy a simple HTTP server in Python using the built-in **http.server** module, developers can use the following command:

bashCopy code

```
python -m http.server
```

This command starts an HTTP server listening on port 8000 by default, serving files from the current directory. Similarly, to make an HTTP request to a server using the **curl** command-line tool, developers can use the following command:

bashCopy code

```
curl http://example.com
```

This command sends an HTTP GET request to the specified URL and prints the response to the console. While HTTP is versatile and widely used, it may not be suitable for all use cases, especially those requiring low latency, high throughput, or real-time communication. In such cases, developers may opt for more specialized communication protocols such as WebSocket or gRPC. WebSocket is a protocol that enables bidirectional, full-duplex communication between clients and servers over a single, long-lived TCP connection. It is well-suited for real-time applications such as chat applications, online gaming, and financial trading platforms, where low latency and high interactivity are critical. Deploying WebSocket-based communication involves setting up WebSocket servers and clients capable of establishing WebSocket connections and exchanging messages in real-time. For example, to deploy a WebSocket server in Node.js using the **ws** library, developers can use the following command:

bashCopy code

```
npm install ws
```

javascriptCopy code

```
const WebSocket = require('ws'); const wss = new
WebSocket.Server({ port: 8080 });
wss.on('connection', function connection(ws) {
ws.on('message', function incoming(message) {
console.log('received: %s', message); });
ws.send('Hello, client!'); });
```

This code sets up a WebSocket server listening on port 8080 and echoes messages received from clients back to them. To connect to this WebSocket server using a WebSocket client, developers can use the **wscat** command-line tool:

bashCopy code

```
npm install -g wscat
```

bashCopy code

```
wscat -c ws://localhost:8080
```

This command establishes a WebSocket connection to the server and allows developers to send and receive messages interactively. gRPC (Google Remote Procedure Call) is another communication protocol gaining popularity, particularly in microservices architectures and cloud-native applications. gRPC is a high-performance, language-agnostic RPC framework that enables efficient communication between services using protocol buffers over HTTP/2. It provides features such as bidirectional streaming, authentication, and automatic client code generation, making it ideal for building distributed systems with complex communication requirements. Deploying gRPC-based communication involves defining service interfaces and methods using Protocol Buffers (.proto files), generating client and server code from these definitions using the **protoc** compiler, and implementing service logic in the generated code. For example, to define a simple gRPC service for a chat application in a .proto file, developers can use the following syntax:

protobufCopy code

```
syntax = "proto3"; service ChatService { rpc
SendMessage (MessageRequest) returns
(MessageResponse) {} } message MessageRequest {
string user = 1; string message = 2; } message
MessageResponse { string status = 1; }
```

This defines a **ChatService** with a single method **SendMessage** that takes a **MessageRequest** and returns a **MessageResponse**. To generate client and server code from this .proto file in Python, developers can use the following command:

bashCopy code

```
python -m grpc_tools.protoc -I. --python_out=. --grpc_python_out=. chat.proto
```

This command generates Python code for the client and server based on the definitions in the .proto file. Developers can then implement the service logic in the generated code and deploy the gRPC server using a suitable deployment mechanism. In summary, choosing the right communication protocol for your use case involves considering factors such as performance, latency, scalability, and ease of implementation. While HTTP is suitable for many applications, WebSocket and gRPC offer specialized features and advantages for real-time communication and microservices architectures, respectively. By understanding the strengths and limitations of each protocol, developers can make informed decisions when designing and implementing communication mechanisms for their distributed systems.

Chapter 3: Microservices Resilience Patterns: Chaos Engineering and Resilience Testing

Chaos Engineering is a discipline that focuses on proactively identifying weaknesses and vulnerabilities in distributed systems by deliberately injecting failures and disruptions into the system to test its resilience and ability to withstand unexpected events. The goal of Chaos Engineering is to uncover weaknesses in a controlled environment before they manifest as costly outages or failures in production. By subjecting systems to controlled chaos, engineers can gain insights into their behavior under adverse conditions and identify areas for improvement. One of the key principles of Chaos Engineering is the concept of "fail fast and recover quickly." This principle emphasizes the importance of detecting failures early and implementing rapid recovery mechanisms to minimize the impact on system performance and availability. To practice Chaos Engineering effectively, engineers must adopt a systematic approach that involves defining steady-state conditions, identifying potential failure modes, designing experiments to simulate those failures, and measuring the system's response to each failure scenario. A popular tool for implementing Chaos Engineering experiments is Chaos Monkey, developed by Netflix. Chaos Monkey is a distributed system resiliency tool that randomly terminates instances and services within a cloud environment to simulate failures and test system resilience. Deploying Chaos Monkey involves configuring it to run within a cloud environment and specifying the scope and frequency of chaos experiments. For example, to deploy Chaos Monkey in an AWS (Amazon Web Services) environment, engineers can use the following command:

bashCopy code

```
aws configure set AWS_ACCESS_KEY_ID <access-key-id> aws configure set AWS_SECRET_ACCESS_KEY <secret-access-key> aws configure set AWS_DEFAULT_REGION <region>
```

This command configures the AWS CLI (Command Line Interface) with the necessary credentials and default region for accessing AWS services. Once configured, engineers can deploy Chaos Monkey using the following command:

bashCopy code

```
chaosmonkey deploy
```

This command starts Chaos Monkey within the AWS environment, where it will randomly terminate instances according to the specified configuration. Another important aspect of Chaos Engineering is the concept of "blast radius," which refers to the extent of the impact caused by a failure or disruption in the system. To mitigate the risk of catastrophic failures, engineers must carefully define the blast radius for each chaos experiment and implement safeguards to limit the scope of potential damage. For example, engineers can use canary deployments and feature flags to gradually roll out changes and limit the impact on production systems. Additionally, engineers must establish clear metrics and monitoring systems to track the impact of chaos experiments on system performance and availability. By measuring key performance indicators such as latency, error rates, and throughput, engineers can assess the effectiveness of their resilience strategies and identify areas for improvement. Implementing Chaos Engineering practices requires collaboration and buy-in from stakeholders across the organization, including developers, operations teams, and business leaders. It is essential to establish a culture of experimentation and learning, where failure is embraced as an opportunity for growth and improvement. By integrating Chaos Engineering into the software development lifecycle, organizations can build more resilient and reliable systems that can withstand the challenges of a dynamic and unpredictable operating environment. In summary, Chaos Engineering is a powerful technique for improving the resilience and reliability of distributed systems by systematically injecting failures and disruptions into the system to test its response. By adopting a disciplined approach to Chaos Engineering and leveraging tools such as Chaos Monkey, organizations can identify weaknesses, improve fault tolerance, and build more robust systems that deliver consistent performance and availability.

Resilience testing is a critical aspect of ensuring the reliability and robustness of microservices architectures, especially in distributed systems where failures are inevitable. Resilience testing involves deliberately introducing faults and failures into a system to evaluate its ability to recover and continue functioning under adverse conditions. By subjecting microservices to various failure scenarios, organizations can identify weaknesses, improve fault tolerance, and enhance overall system resilience. One common resilience testing strategy is fault injection, where faults such as network latency, packet loss, or service unavailability are injected into the system to observe how it responds. Tools like Chaos Monkey, Gremlin, and Pumba enable engineers to inject faults into microservices environments easily. For example, to simulate network latency using Gremlin, engineers can use the following CLI command:

bashCopy code

```
gremlin latency --host <service-host> --time 500 --duration 60
```

This command injects a network latency of 500 milliseconds into the specified service for a duration of 60 seconds. By injecting faults selectively and observing the system's behavior, engineers can gain insights into its resilience mechanisms and identify potential areas for improvement. Another resilience testing strategy is the use of fault tolerance patterns such as circuit breakers, retries, and fallback mechanisms. Circuit breakers, for example, prevent cascading failures by temporarily blocking requests to a service that is experiencing issues. To test the effectiveness of circuit breakers, engineers can intentionally overload a service and observe how the circuit breaker reacts. For example, using the Hystrix library in Java, engineers can configure a circuit breaker with the following command: javaCopy code

```
HystrixCommand.Setter.withCircuitBreakerEnabled( tru
e)    .withCircuitBreakerErrorThresholdPercentage( 50 )
.withCircuitBreakerRequestVolumeThreshold( 20 )
.withCircuitBreakerSleepWindowInMilliseconds( 5000 );
```

This configuration sets the circuit breaker to open if the error threshold exceeds 50% or if the number of requests exceeds 20 within a 5-second window. By testing circuit breakers under load, engineers can validate their effectiveness in preventing service degradation and promoting system stability. Additionally, chaos engineering techniques such as game days and failure injection testing can help organizations simulate real-world failure scenarios and assess their impact on system performance and availability. Game days involve organizing structured events where teams simulate failure scenarios and work together to restore service functionality. These events allow organizations to validate incident response procedures, train personnel, and improve overall system resilience. Failure injection testing, on the other hand, involves systematically injecting failures into a production environment to test the system's resilience. For example, engineers can use the Chaos Toolkit to define and execute failure injection experiments using YAML-based configuration files:

yamlCopy code

```
configuration: steady-state-hypothesis: title: Service
is operational probes: - name: service-availability
type: probe tolerance: - tolerated: true method: -
type: action name: failure-injection provider: type:
python module: chaosaws.network.actions func:
"latency" arguments: action: introduce-latency
resource_type: "ec2_instance" region: "us-west-2"
filters: "tag:Name": "my-service" latency: 2000
duration: 60
```

This configuration introduces network latency of 2000 milliseconds into the specified EC2 instance in the US West 2 region for a duration of 60 seconds. By executing such experiments in a controlled manner, organizations can validate their resilience strategies and identify areas for improvement. In summary, resilience testing is essential for validating the reliability and robustness of microservices architectures. By employing fault injection, fault tolerance patterns, chaos engineering techniques, and structured testing approaches, organizations can enhance their ability to withstand failures and ensure the uninterrupted delivery of services to users. By making resilience testing an integral part of the software development lifecycle, organizations can build more resilient, reliable, and scalable microservices architectures that meet the demands of modern, distributed applications.

Chapter 4: Fine-Tuning Microservices for Performance: Caching and Data Access Optimization

Distributed caching is a fundamental technique used in microservices architectures to improve performance, scalability, and resilience by storing frequently accessed data in memory across multiple nodes in a distributed environment. By caching data closer to the application, distributed caching reduces the latency associated with accessing data from remote data sources such as databases or external APIs. Additionally, distributed caching helps alleviate the load on backend systems by serving cached data directly from memory, thereby improving overall system throughput and responsiveness. One of the most widely used distributed caching solutions is Redis, a high-performance, in-memory data store that supports various data structures such as strings, lists, sets, and hashes. To deploy Redis in a distributed architecture, organizations can use container orchestration platforms like Kubernetes to deploy Redis as a stateful set. The following CLI command can be used to deploy a Redis stateful set in Kubernetes:

bashCopy code

```
kubectl apply -f redis-statefulset.yaml
```

This command applies the configuration defined in the **redis-statefulset.yaml** file, which specifies the desired state of the Redis stateful set, including the number of replicas, resource requirements, and storage configuration. Once deployed, Redis instances can be accessed by microservices within the Kubernetes cluster, allowing them to store and retrieve cached data efficiently. Another popular distributed caching solution is Memcached, a high-performance, distributed memory object caching system. Memcached is commonly used to cache the results of expensive computations or database queries to improve application performance. To deploy Memcached in a distributed environment, organizations can use container orchestration platforms like Docker Swarm to deploy Memcached as a service. The following CLI command can be used to deploy Memcached as a service in Docker Swarm:

bashCopy code

```
docker service create --name memcached --replicas 3
memcached:latest
```

This command creates a Memcached service with three replicas, ensuring high availability and fault tolerance. Each Memcached instance can be accessed by microservices running on the Docker Swarm cluster, allowing them to store and retrieve cached data efficiently. In addition to Redis and Memcached, there are several other distributed caching solutions available, each with its own strengths and weaknesses. For example, Apache Ignite is a distributed in-memory computing platform that provides caching, compute, and streaming capabilities. Apache Ignite is often used in scenarios where both caching and compute capabilities are required, such as real-time analytics and machine learning inference. To deploy Apache Ignite in a distributed architecture, organizations can use tools like Apache Mesos or Kubernetes to deploy Ignite as a cluster. The following CLI command can be used to deploy Apache Ignite as a cluster in Kubernetes:

bashCopy code

```
kubectl apply -f ignite-cluster.yaml
```

This command applies the configuration defined in the **ignite-cluster.yaml** file, which specifies the desired state of the Ignite cluster, including the number of nodes, resource requirements, and network configuration. Once deployed, Apache Ignite provides a distributed caching layer that can be accessed by microservices to store and retrieve cached data efficiently. When implementing distributed caching strategies, organizations must consider several factors, including data consistency, eviction policies, and cache invalidation mechanisms. Depending on the requirements of the application, organizations may choose different caching strategies such as write-through caching, write-behind caching, or read-through caching. Write-through caching involves writing data to both the cache and the underlying data source simultaneously, ensuring that the cache remains consistent with the data source. To implement write-through caching, organizations can use libraries like Spring Cache with Redis or Memcached to automatically cache method results and synchronize them with the underlying data source. The following Java code snippet demonstrates how to configure write-through caching with Spring Cache and Redis:

javaCopy code

```
@Cacheable(value = "books", key = "#isbn") public
Book findBookByIsbn(String isbn) { return
bookRepository.findByIsbn(isbn); } @CachePut(value =
"books", key = "#book.isbn") public Book
updateBook(Book book) { return
bookRepository.save(book); }
```

In this example, the **findBookByIsbn** method retrieves a book from the cache using the specified ISBN key. If the book is not found in the cache, it is retrieved from the underlying data source (e.g., a database) and stored in the cache for future access. The **updateBook** method updates a book in the cache and the underlying data source simultaneously, ensuring that both remain consistent. Write-behind caching, on the other hand, involves writing data to the cache first and asynchronously propagating the changes to the underlying data source. This approach improves write performance by reducing the latency associated with writing to the data source. To implement write-behind caching, organizations can use libraries like Apache Ignite or Hazelcast to buffer write operations in memory and periodically flush them to the data source. The following configuration demonstrates how to enable write-behind caching with Apache Ignite:

```
xmlCopy code
<bean                          id="cacheConfiguration"
class="org.apache.ignite.configuration.CacheConfigurati
on">      <property    name="name"    value="books"/>
<property name="cacheMode" value="PARTITIONED"/>
<property     name="writeThrough"     value="false"/>
```

```xml
<property name="writeBehindEnabled" value="true"/>
<property name="writeBehindFlushSize" value="100"/>
<property name="writeBehindFlushFrequency" value="5000"/> </bean>
```

In this configuration, the **writeThrough** property is set to **false** to disable write-through caching, while the **writeBehindEnabled** property is set to **true** to enable write-behind caching. The **writeBehindFlushSize** property specifies the maximum number of write operations to buffer before flushing them to the data source, while the **writeBehindFlushFrequency** property specifies the frequency (in milliseconds) at which buffered writes are flushed to the data source. Finally, read-through caching involves automatically loading data into the cache from the underlying data source when it is requested by a client. This approach ensures that cached data is always up-to-date and consistent with the data source. To implement read-through caching, organizations can use libraries like Ehcache or Guava Cache to define cache loaders that automatically fetch data from the data source when it is requested. The following Java code snippet demonstrates how to configure read-through caching with Ehcache:

```java
javaCopy code
CacheManager           cacheManager            =
CacheManagerBuilder.newCacheManagerBuilder()
.withCache("books",
CacheConfigurationBuilder.newCacheConfigurationBuil
der(                Long.class,               Book.class,
ResourcePoolsBuilder.heap(100))
```

```
.withLoaderWriter( new      BookCacheLoaderWriter())
.build()) .build( true);
```
In this code snippet, a cache manager is created with a cache named "books" that uses a **BookCacheLoaderWriter** to load data from the underlying data source when it is requested. By using caching strategies such as write-through, write-behind, and read-through, organizations can effectively manage data consistency and performance in distributed microservices architectures. Additionally, organizations must carefully consider cache eviction policies and cache invalidation mechanisms to ensure that cached data remains relevant and up-to-date. Eviction policies determine when cached entries are removed from the cache to free up memory and prevent memory exhaustion. Common eviction policies include time-based eviction, size-based eviction, and least recently used (LRU) eviction. Time-based eviction removes entries from the cache after a specified period of time has elapsed since they were last accessed or inserted. To configure time-based eviction with Redis, organizations can use the **EXPIRE** command to set a time-to-live (TTL) for cached keys:

bashCopy code

```
SET mykey "myvalue" EX 3600
```

This command sets the value of the **mykey** key to "myvalue" with an expiration time of 3600 seconds (1 hour). After 1 hour, the key is automatically removed from the cache, ensuring that cached data remains fresh and up-to-date. Size-based eviction removes entries from the cache when the cache reaches a certain size threshold, preventing memory exhaustion and cache thrashing. To implement size-based eviction with Memcached, organizations can use the **maxbytes** parameter to limit the total size of the cache:

bashCopy code

```
docker run -d --name memcached -p 11211:11211 memcached:latest -m 64
```

This command starts a Memcached container with a maximum memory limit of 64 megabytes. When the cache reaches this limit, Memcached automatically evicts entries using a least recently used (LRU) eviction strategy to make room for new entries. LRU eviction removes the least recently accessed entries from the cache when the cache reaches its size limit, ensuring that the most frequently accessed data remains in the cache. To configure LRU eviction with Redis, organizations can use the **MAXMEMORY** and **MAXMEMORY_POLICY** parameters to specify the maximum memory limit and eviction policy, respectively:

bashCopy code

```
docker run -d --name redis -p 6379:6379 redis:latest --maxmemory 64mb --maxmemory-policy allkeys-lru
```

This command starts a Redis container with a maximum memory limit of 64 megabytes and an LRU eviction policy. When the cache reaches its memory limit, Redis automatically evicts the least recently used keys from the cache to free up memory for new entries. In summary, distributed caching is a powerful technique for improving performance, scalability, and resilience in microservices architectures. By caching frequently accessed data in memory across multiple nodes, organizations can reduce latency, alleviate backend load, and improve overall system throughput. By carefully selecting caching strategies, eviction policies, and cache invalidation mechanisms, organizations can ensure that cached data remains relevant, consistent, and up-to-date, enabling them to deliver fast and reliable services to users.

Database sharding and replication are two essential techniques used in distributed systems to improve performance, scalability, and availability. Sharding involves partitioning a large database into smaller, more manageable fragments called shards, distributed across multiple servers or nodes. Each shard contains a subset of the data and operates independently, allowing for parallel processing and improved read and write throughput. Replication, on the other hand, involves creating and maintaining multiple copies of the data across different nodes to increase fault tolerance and reduce latency. By combining sharding and replication, organizations can achieve significant performance improvements in their distributed systems.

To implement database sharding, organizations first need to determine an appropriate sharding key, which is used to partition the data across shards. Common sharding keys include customer ID, geographical location, or timestamp, depending on the nature of the application and access patterns. Once the sharding key is chosen, organizations can use database management systems like MongoDB or MySQL to create sharded clusters and distribute the data across shards. For example, in MongoDB, the following CLI command can be used to enable sharding for a specific collection:

bashCopy code

```
sh.shardCollection("testDB.testCollection",          {
"shardingKey": 1 })
```

This command shards the **testCollection** collection in the **testDB** database based on the **shardingKey** field. MongoDB then automatically distributes the data across shards based on the values of the sharding key, allowing for horizontal scaling and improved performance.

In addition to sharding, database replication is another critical technique used to improve performance and availability. Database replication involves creating and maintaining multiple copies of the data across different nodes, ensuring that updates made to one copy are propagated to all other copies. This allows for load balancing, fault tolerance, and disaster recovery in distributed systems. To implement database replication, organizations can use features provided by database management systems such as MySQL's built-in replication capabilities. The following CLI commands demonstrate how to set up replication in MySQL:

bashCopy code

```
mysql>      CHANGE      MASTER      TO      ->
MASTER_HOST='master.example.com',              ->
MASTER_USER='replication_user',                ->
MASTER_PASSWORD='password',                    ->
MASTER_LOG_FILE='mysql-bin.000001',            ->
MASTER_LOG_POS=107; mysql> START SLAVE;
```

These commands configure a MySQL slave server to replicate data from a master server located at **master.example.com**. The **CHANGE MASTER TO** statement specifies the master server's connection details, including the host, username, password, and binary log file position. Once configured, the **START SLAVE** statement starts the replication process, allowing the slave server to receive and apply updates from the master server.

By combining sharding and replication, organizations can achieve even greater performance improvements in their distributed systems. Sharding allows for horizontal scaling by distributing the data across multiple shards, while replication provides fault tolerance and high availability by maintaining multiple copies of the data. Together, these techniques enable organizations to build scalable, resilient, and high-performance distributed databases that can handle the demands of modern applications.

However, implementing database sharding and replication also introduces challenges and considerations that organizations must address. One challenge is data consistency, as updates made to one shard or replica must be propagated to all other shards or replicas to ensure consistency across the database. This requires careful coordination and synchronization mechanisms to handle conflicts and resolve inconsistencies. Additionally, organizations must consider the impact of sharding and replication on application architecture, query routing, and data migration strategies. Complexities such as data skew, hotspots, and cross-shard transactions can arise and require careful planning and optimization to mitigate.

Despite these challenges, database sharding and replication remain powerful techniques for improving performance, scalability, and availability in distributed systems. By carefully designing and implementing sharded and replicated databases, organizations can build robust and scalable architectures capable of supporting the growing demands of modern applications and users.

In summary, database sharding and replication are essential techniques for improving performance and scalability in distributed systems. Sharding allows for horizontal scaling by partitioning the data across multiple shards, while replication provides fault tolerance and high availability by maintaining multiple copies of the data. By combining these techniques, organizations can build distributed databases that are capable of handling the demands of modern applications and users. However, implementing sharding and replication introduces challenges such as data consistency, query routing, and data migration, which must be carefully addressed to ensure success. Despite these challenges, database sharding and replication remain powerful tools for building scalable, resilient, and high-performance distributed systems.

Chapter 5: Advanced Security Measures for Microservices: Encryption and Tokenization

End-to-end encryption (E2EE) is a crucial security measure employed in microservices architectures to protect sensitive data as it travels between different services within the system. E2EE ensures that data is encrypted at the source and can only be decrypted by the intended recipient, preventing unauthorized access or interception by malicious actors. In the context of microservices, where communication often occurs over untrusted networks such as the internet or cloud, E2EE plays a vital role in safeguarding data privacy and confidentiality.

To implement E2EE in microservices communication, organizations can use various cryptographic algorithms and protocols to encrypt and decrypt data securely. One widely adopted approach is the use of asymmetric encryption, where each service possesses a public-private key pair. The public key is used for encryption, while the private key is used for decryption. This ensures that only authorized recipients with access to the corresponding private key can decrypt the data. For example, in a scenario where Service A needs to send encrypted data to Service B, Service A encrypts the data using Service B's public key before transmitting it over the network:

bashCopy code

```
openssl rsautl -encrypt -in plaintext.txt -out encrypted.txt -pubin -inkey public_key.pem
```

In this command, **openssl** is a command-line tool for cryptographic operations, **rsautl** is the command for RSA encryption and decryption, **-encrypt** specifies that the operation is encryption, **-in plaintext.txt** specifies the input file containing the plaintext data, **-out encrypted.txt** specifies the output file for the encrypted data, **-pubin** indicates that the input key is a public key, and **-inkey public_key.pem** specifies the file containing the public key of Service B.

On the receiving end, Service B decrypts the encrypted data using its private key:

bashCopy code

```
openssl rsautl -decrypt -in encrypted.txt -out decrypted.txt -inkey private_key.pem
```

In this command, **-decrypt** indicates that the operation is decryption, **-in encrypted.txt** specifies the input file containing the encrypted data, **-out decrypted.txt** specifies the output file for the decrypted plaintext, and **-inkey private_key.pem** specifies the file containing the private key of Service B.

Another approach to implementing E2EE in microservices communication is the use of symmetric encryption, where both the sender and the receiver share a secret key for encryption and decryption. While symmetric encryption is faster and more efficient than asymmetric encryption, it requires a secure mechanism for key distribution and management. One common method is the use of key management services or dedicated key management systems to securely generate, distribute, and rotate encryption keys among microservices.

In addition to encryption, organizations must also consider key management, authentication, and authorization mechanisms to ensure the security and integrity of microservices communication. Key management involves securely storing and managing encryption keys, including key generation, rotation, and revocation. Authentication ensures that only authorized services can access and decrypt data, while authorization controls the actions and permissions of authenticated services based on predefined policies and roles.

To further enhance security, organizations can implement mutual TLS (mTLS) authentication, where both the client and the server authenticate each other using digital certificates. mTLS provides an additional layer of security by verifying the identities of both parties involved in the communication, preventing man-in-the-middle attacks and unauthorized access. To deploy mTLS in microservices communication, organizations can use tools like OpenSSL to generate and manage digital certificates for client and server authentication:

bashCopy code

```
openssl genrsa -out server.key 2048 openssl req -new -key server.key -out server.csr openssl x509 -req -in server.csr -CA ca.crt -CAkey ca.key -CAcreateserial -out server.crt -days 365
```

In this sequence of commands, **openssl genrsa** generates a private key for the server, **openssl req** generates a certificate signing request (CSR) for the server, and **openssl x509** signs the CSR with a certificate authority (CA) to generate a digital certificate for the server. Similar steps can be followed to generate client certificates for mutual authentication.

By implementing E2EE, organizations can ensure that sensitive data remains protected throughout its journey across microservices within the system. Whether using asymmetric or symmetric encryption, along with robust key management and authentication mechanisms, E2EE plays a critical role in maintaining data privacy, confidentiality, and integrity in distributed microservices architectures.

Tokenization techniques for data protection are crucial in modern computing environments, especially in scenarios where sensitive information needs to be securely stored, processed, and transmitted. Tokenization involves replacing sensitive data elements with non-sensitive placeholder tokens, which retain the format and length of the original data but are devoid of any meaningful information. This approach helps mitigate the risk of data breaches and unauthorized access, as even if a token is intercepted or compromised, it does not reveal any sensitive information.

One common application of tokenization is in payment processing systems, where credit card numbers are replaced with tokens to facilitate transactions without exposing the actual card details. The process typically involves a tokenization service that generates and manages unique tokens for each sensitive data element, such as credit card numbers, social security numbers, or personally identifiable information (PII).

To tokenize sensitive data, organizations can leverage various tokenization techniques, including format-preserving encryption (FPE), random token generation, and token vaults. Format-preserving encryption is a cryptographic technique that encrypts data while preserving its original format, such as maintaining the length and character set of credit card numbers. This ensures compatibility with existing systems and processes while enhancing security.

Random token generation involves generating unique tokens for sensitive data elements using cryptographic algorithms or pseudo-random number generators (PRNGs). These tokens have no inherent relationship with the original data, making them difficult to reverse-engineer or decipher. Token vaults are secure storage repositories that maintain mappings between original data elements and their corresponding tokens.

For example, in a payment processing system, sensitive cardholder data can be tokenized using a tokenization service:

bashCopy code

```
curl -X POST https://api.tokenization-service.com/tokenize \ -H 'Content-Type: application/json' \ -d '{ "credit_card_number": "1234567812345678", "expiration_date": "12/23", "cvv": "123" }'
```

In this command, **curl** is a command-line tool for making HTTP requests, **-X POST** specifies the HTTP method as POST, **-H 'Content-Type: application/json'** sets the request header to indicate JSON data, and **-d** sends the JSON payload containing the sensitive credit card details to the tokenization service endpoint.

The tokenization service then generates a unique token for the credit card number and returns it as a response: jsonCopy code

{ "token": "eyJhbGciOiJIUzI1NiIsInR5cCI6IkpXVCJ9.eyJjcmVkaXQiOiJ0b2tlbi1kYXRhLWluZm8iLCJleHBpcmF0aW9uX2RhdGUiOilyMDIzLTEyLTIzVDEyOjIzOjQwLjIzNFoiLCJjdXYiOilxMjM0NTY3ODEyMzQ1Njc4OSIsIm42dil6IjEyMyJ9.GyOwN8a6W4WdpUCxLy0OQliXjb_e4HGMzWMLH7T2qsw" }

This token can then be used in subsequent transactions or operations within the system, eliminating the need to store or transmit sensitive cardholder data.

Tokenization techniques provide several benefits for data protection and compliance, including reducing the scope of regulatory requirements such as the Payment Card Industry Data Security Standard (PCI DSS) and the General Data Protection Regulation (GDPR). By tokenizing sensitive data, organizations can minimize the risk of data breaches, streamline compliance efforts, and enhance customer trust and confidence in their services. Moreover, tokenization supports secure data sharing and collaboration across different systems and organizations without compromising data security or integrity.

In addition to protecting sensitive data at rest and in transit, organizations must also implement robust access controls, encryption, and monitoring mechanisms to safeguard tokenization processes and token vaults from unauthorized access or tampering. By adopting a comprehensive approach to data protection and security, organizations can effectively mitigate risks and vulnerabilities associated with handling sensitive information in today's interconnected and data-driven environments.

Chapter 6: Implementing Role-Based Access Control (RBAC) in Microservices Architecture

Role-Based Access Control (RBAC) is a widely adopted approach to managing access to resources within an organization's information systems. RBAC provides a structured method for assigning permissions to users based on their roles and responsibilities, rather than individual identities. This approach enhances security, simplifies administration, and promotes scalability by centralizing access control decisions.

At the core of RBAC are three fundamental concepts: roles, permissions, and users. Roles represent a collection of permissions that are associated with specific job functions or responsibilities within the organization. Permissions define the actions or operations that users can perform on resources, such as read, write, or execute. Users are individuals or entities granted access to the system and assigned one or more roles based on their job requirements.

To implement RBAC, organizations first define roles and their corresponding permissions. This process involves identifying distinct job functions or responsibilities within the organization and determining the appropriate set of permissions associated with each role. For example, in a healthcare organization, roles such as physician, nurse, and administrator may have different sets of permissions based on their respective duties.

Once roles and permissions are defined, organizations assign users to roles based on their job roles or responsibilities. This assignment process can be manual or automated, depending on the size and complexity of the organization. In some cases, users may be assigned multiple roles to accommodate varying job functions or project requirements.

bashCopy code

```
kubectl create rolebinding developer-rolebinding --clusterrole=edit --user=user@example.com
```

In this command, **kubectl create rolebinding** is used to create a role binding, **developer-rolebinding** is the name of the role binding being created, **--clusterrole=edit** specifies the cluster role being assigned, and **--user=user@example.com** specifies the user to whom the role is being assigned.

RBAC implementations typically support role inheritance and role hierarchies, allowing roles to inherit permissions from other roles or be organized into hierarchical structures. This flexibility enables organizations to define granular access control policies that align with their business requirements and organizational structure.

Another important aspect of RBAC is role activation and deactivation. Organizations often need to activate or deactivate roles for users based on changes in job roles, project assignments, or employee status. Role activation involves granting access to resources associated with a specific role, while role deactivation revokes access for users who no longer require it.

RBAC also supports the concept of least privilege, which stipulates that users should be granted the minimum level of access required to perform their job functions effectively. This principle helps minimize the risk of unauthorized access and reduces the potential impact of security breaches or insider threats.

To enforce RBAC policies, organizations deploy access control mechanisms at various layers of their IT infrastructure, including operating systems, databases, applications, and network devices. Role-based access control is often implemented using access control lists (ACLs), directory services such as Active Directory or LDAP, or specialized identity and access management (IAM) solutions.

RBAC implementations should also include mechanisms for auditing and logging access control decisions to ensure compliance with regulatory requirements and internal policies. Auditing capabilities enable organizations to track user activity, monitor access patterns, and detect anomalous behavior that may indicate unauthorized access or misuse of privileges.

In summary, Role-Based Access Control (RBAC) is a foundational principle in modern information security, providing a structured and scalable approach to managing access to resources. By defining roles, permissions, and user assignments, organizations can effectively control access to sensitive data and critical systems while promoting operational efficiency and compliance with regulatory requirements. Deploying RBAC requires careful planning, documentation, and ongoing management to ensure its effectiveness and alignment with organizational goals and objectives.

Role-Based Access Control (RBAC) is a crucial component of microservices environments, providing a structured method for managing access to resources and ensuring the principle of least privilege. In microservices architectures, where numerous services interact with each other and access shared resources, implementing RBAC effectively is essential to maintaining security and enforcing access control policies. Several best practices can help organizations optimize their RBAC implementations in microservices environments.

First and foremost, organizations should adopt a fine-grained approach to RBAC, defining roles and permissions at a granular level to align with the specific needs of microservices. Rather than creating broad roles with extensive permissions, organizations should aim for role granularity, assigning permissions based on the principle of least privilege. This approach minimizes the risk of unauthorized access and reduces the potential impact of security breaches.

bashCopy code

```
kubectl create role developer-role --verb=get,list,create
--resource=pods
```

In this command, **kubectl create role** is used to create a role named **developer-role**, **--verb=get,list,create** specifies the permissions associated with the role, and -**-resource=pods** defines the resource to which the permissions apply.

Another best practice is to establish clear naming conventions for roles and permissions to ensure consistency and manageability. By using descriptive names for roles and permissions, organizations can easily understand their purpose and scope, facilitating role assignment and administration.

Organizations should also implement role hierarchies and role inheritance where appropriate. Role hierarchies enable roles to inherit permissions from other roles, simplifying role management and reducing the need for manual assignment of permissions. This approach can be particularly beneficial in complex microservices environments with numerous roles and permissions.

RBAC policies should be regularly reviewed and updated to reflect changes in organizational roles, responsibilities, and access requirements. Regular audits of RBAC configurations help identify inconsistencies, unauthorized access, and potential security vulnerabilities. Automated tools and scripts can assist in performing RBAC audits and identifying discrepancies in role assignments and permissions.

Organizations should enforce the principle of least privilege by regularly reviewing and pruning unnecessary permissions from roles. Periodic access reviews help ensure that users have only the permissions necessary to perform their job functions, reducing the attack surface and mitigating the risk of insider threats.

RBAC policies should be integrated into the continuous integration and continuous deployment (CI/CD) pipeline to enforce security and compliance throughout the software development lifecycle. Automated deployment scripts and configuration management tools can help ensure that RBAC policies are consistently applied across development, testing, and production environments.

Centralized management of RBAC policies is essential in microservices environments, where multiple services may require access to shared resources. Organizations should consider using centralized identity and access management (IAM) solutions to manage RBAC policies centrally and enforce consistent access control across all microservices.

RBAC should be complemented with robust authentication mechanisms, such as multi-factor authentication (MFA), to enhance security and prevent unauthorized access. Organizations should also implement strong encryption protocols to protect sensitive data and communications between microservices.

Monitoring and logging of RBAC activities are critical for detecting and responding to security incidents promptly. Organizations should implement robust logging mechanisms to record user access, permission changes, and authentication events. Security information and event management (SIEM) systems can help aggregate and analyze log data to identify potential security threats and policy violations.

In summary, implementing RBAC best practices is essential for ensuring security and compliance in microservices environments. By adopting a fine-grained approach to RBAC, establishing clear naming conventions, implementing role hierarchies, and regularly auditing RBAC policies, organizations can strengthen their security posture and mitigate the risk of unauthorized access. Integrating RBAC into the CI/CD pipeline, centralizing RBAC management, and implementing robust authentication and encryption mechanisms further enhance security in microservices environments. Monitoring and logging RBAC activities enable organizations to detect and respond to security incidents promptly, ensuring the integrity and confidentiality of microservices-based applications.

Chapter 7: Secure Service-to-Service Communication with Mutual TLS (mTLS)

Mutual Transport Layer Security (mTLS) is a security protocol that ensures the integrity, authenticity, and confidentiality of communication between client and server applications in a microservices environment. Unlike traditional TLS, where only the server presents a certificate to authenticate itself to the client, mTLS requires both the client and server to present certificates, enabling mutual authentication. This additional layer of security helps prevent man-in-the-middle attacks and unauthorized access to sensitive data.

To configure and set up mTLS in a microservices environment, several steps need to be followed. Firstly, organizations must generate and manage digital certificates for both clients and servers. These certificates include public and private keys used for encryption and authentication purposes. Organizations can use tools like OpenSSL to generate certificate signing requests (CSRs) and create self-signed certificates or obtain certificates from a trusted certificate authority (CA).

bashCopy code

```
openssl req -new -newkey rsa:2048 -nodes -keyout server.key -out server.csr
```

In this command, **openssl req** is used to generate a new certificate signing request (CSR) and private key (**server.key**), and the resulting CSR is saved to **server.csr**.

Once the certificates are generated, organizations need to configure their microservices applications to use mTLS for secure communication. This involves updating the application code or configuration to enable TLS encryption and mutual authentication. Most modern programming languages and frameworks provide libraries and modules for implementing mTLS, simplifying the integration process.

```python
pythonCopy code
import ssl context = ssl.create_default_context(ssl.Purpose.CLIENT_AUTH)
context.load_cert_chain(certfile="client.crt", keyfile="client.key")
```

In this Python code snippet, an SSL context is created with **ssl.create_default_context()**, and the client's certificate and private key are loaded using **context.load_cert_chain()**.

Organizations should also configure their microservices deployment infrastructure, such as container orchestration platforms like Kubernetes, to support mTLS. This involves configuring ingress controllers, load balancers, and service meshes to terminate TLS connections and enforce mutual authentication between client and server components.

```yaml
yamlCopy code
apiVersion: networking.k8s.io/v1 kind: Ingress metadata: name: example-ingress spec: tls: - hosts: - example.com secretName: tls-secret
```

In this Kubernetes manifest, an Ingress resource is configured with TLS termination using a secret named **tls-secret**, which contains the server's certificate and private key.

Furthermore, organizations should establish trust relationships between client and server certificates to ensure secure communication. This involves configuring certificate authorities (CAs) and certificate trust stores to validate the authenticity of certificates presented during the mTLS handshake. Organizations can deploy internal CAs or utilize third-party CA services for certificate issuance and management.

bashCopy code

```
kubectl create secret tls tls-secret --cert=server.crt --key=server.key
```

In this Kubernetes command, a TLS secret named **tls-secret** is created using the server's certificate (**server.crt**) and private key (**server.key**).

Once mTLS is configured and deployed, organizations should monitor and maintain their mTLS infrastructure to ensure continued security and compliance. This includes regularly updating certificates, rotating cryptographic keys, and monitoring mTLS handshake failures and certificate revocations for signs of potential security incidents.

In summary, configuring and setting up mutual TLS (mTLS) in a microservices environment is essential for ensuring secure communication between client and server applications. By generating and managing digital certificates, configuring microservices applications and deployment infrastructure, establishing trust relationships, and implementing monitoring and maintenance practices, organizations can enhance the security and integrity of their microservices-based architectures.

Managing certificates and key rotation in microservices is a critical aspect of maintaining the security and integrity of a distributed system. In a microservices architecture, each service typically requires its own set of certificates and cryptographic keys for securing communication channels and verifying the identity of endpoints. These certificates and keys need to be carefully managed and rotated periodically to mitigate security risks and comply with industry regulations and best practices.

To effectively manage certificates and keys in a microservices environment, organizations should establish robust processes and implement appropriate tools for certificate generation, distribution, rotation, and revocation. One commonly used tool for managing certificates is OpenSSL, a versatile command-line tool that provides various cryptographic functions and utilities for working with certificates and keys.

bashCopy code

```
openssl genrsa -out server.key 2048
```

This command generates a new RSA private key (**server.key**) with a key size of 2048 bits using OpenSSL.

Once the private key is generated, organizations can use it to create a certificate signing request (CSR) that will be used to obtain a digital certificate from a certificate authority (CA).

bashCopy code

```
openssl req -new -key server.key -out server.csr
```

In this command, OpenSSL is used to generate a new CSR (**server.csr**) using the private key (**server.key**) created earlier.

After generating the CSR, organizations can submit it to a trusted CA or an internal certificate authority for signing. The CA will validate the CSR and issue a digital certificate that binds the public key to the identity of the service.

bashCopy code

```
openssl x509 -req -in server.csr -CA ca.crt -CAkey ca.key -CAcreateserial -out server.crt -days 365
```

This command creates a new X.509 certificate (**server.crt**) by signing the CSR (**server.csr**) using a CA certificate (**ca.crt**) and its private key (**ca.key**). The resulting certificate is valid for 365 days.

Once the certificate is obtained, it needs to be deployed to the appropriate microservices components, such as load balancers, ingress controllers, and service meshes, to enable secure communication.

bashCopy code

```
kubectl create secret tls tls-secret --cert=server.crt --key=server.key
```

In this Kubernetes command, a TLS secret named **tls-secret** is created using the server's certificate (**server.crt**) and private key (**server.key**).

In addition to initial certificate deployment, organizations must establish processes for certificate rotation to ensure that cryptographic keys are regularly updated to mitigate the risk of compromise due to key theft or cryptographic vulnerabilities. Key rotation involves generating new key pairs and obtaining fresh certificates from the CA, followed by updating the deployed certificates on microservices components.

bashCopy code

```
openssl genrsa -out server-new.key 2048 openssl req -new -key server-new.key -out server-new.csr openssl x509 -req -in server-new.csr -CA ca.crt -CAkey ca.key -CAcreateserial -out server-new.crt -days 365 kubectl create secret tls tls-secret --cert=server-new.crt --key=server-new.key
```

In this example, a new private key (**server-new.key**) and CSR (**server-new.csr**) are generated, and a new certificate (**server-new.crt**) is issued by the CA. The TLS secret **tls-secret** is then updated with the new certificate and key.

Automating certificate management and key rotation processes is essential for maintaining security and operational efficiency in a microservices environment. Organizations can leverage tools such as HashiCorp Vault, cert-manager, or custom scripts to automate certificate lifecycle management, including issuance, renewal, and revocation.

By implementing robust processes and leveraging automation tools, organizations can effectively manage certificates and key rotation in their microservices architectures, enhancing security and compliance posture while minimizing operational overhead.

Chapter 8: Microservices Security Best Practices: Threat Modeling and Vulnerability Management

Threat modeling is a crucial aspect of designing secure microservices architectures, helping organizations identify potential security threats and vulnerabilities early in the development process. By systematically analyzing potential attack vectors and mitigating risks, threat modeling enables organizations to build more resilient and secure microservices applications. Several techniques and methodologies can be employed to conduct threat modeling in microservices environments, each offering unique perspectives on identifying and addressing security concerns.

One widely used threat modeling technique is the STRIDE model, which provides a systematic framework for categorizing potential threats based on six categories: Spoofing, Tampering, Repudiation, Information Disclosure, Denial of Service, and Elevation of Privilege. Using the STRIDE model, organizations can systematically analyze each component of their microservices architecture to identify potential security vulnerabilities and develop appropriate countermeasures.

plaintextCopy code

STRIDE Analysis: 1. Spoofing: Verify authentication mechanisms to prevent unauthorized access to microservices. 2. Tampering: Ensure data integrity by implementing secure communication protocols and input validation. 3. Repudiation: Implement robust logging and auditing mechanisms to track user actions and detect potential fraud. 4. Information Disclosure: Encrypt sensitive data at rest and in transit to prevent unauthorized access. 5. Denial of Service: Implement rate limiting, request throttling, and DDoS protection mechanisms to mitigate the impact of denial-of-service attacks. 6. Elevation of Privilege: Enforce least privilege access control policies and regularly review permissions to prevent unauthorized escalation of privileges.

Another widely used threat modeling technique is the DREAD model, which assesses threats based on five dimensions: Damage potential, Reproducibility, Exploitability, Affected users, and Discoverability. By evaluating each dimension for potential threats, organizations can prioritize security vulnerabilities based on their potential impact and likelihood of exploitation.

plaintextCopy code

DREAD Analysis: 1. Damage Potential: Assess the potential impact of a security vulnerability on the confidentiality, integrity, and availability of microservices. 2. Reproducibility: Determine the ease with which an attacker can reproduce the exploit and exploitability. 3. Exploitability: Evaluate the likelihood that an attacker can exploit the vulnerability given the current security controls and attack vectors. 4. Affected Users: Identify the number and types of users affected by the security vulnerability, including internal users, customers, and third-party integrations. 5. Discoverability: Assess the ease with which an attacker can discover the vulnerability through automated scanning, manual inspection, or public disclosure.

In addition to the STRIDE and DREAD models, organizations can leverage threat modeling methodologies such as attack trees, data flow diagrams, and misuse cases to identify and prioritize security threats in microservices architectures. Attack trees enable organizations to systematically analyze potential attack scenarios and identify the critical paths that attackers may exploit to compromise the system.

```
plaintextCopy code
Attack Tree Example: 1. Unauthorized Access - Brute Force Authentication - Exploit Vulnerable Authentication Mechanism 2. Data Breach - SQL Injection Attack - Cross-Site Scripting (XSS) 3. Denial of Service - Distributed Denial of Service (DDoS) Attack - Resource Exhaustion Attack
```

Data flow diagrams help organizations visualize the flow of sensitive data within microservices architectures and identify potential points of data leakage or unauthorized access. By mapping data flows and access controls, organizations can better understand the security implications of their microservices design decisions.

Misuse cases complement traditional use cases by identifying potential misuse scenarios and abuse cases that adversaries may exploit to compromise the security of microservices applications. By considering how attackers may misuse legitimate functionalities and features, organizations can better prioritize security requirements and implement appropriate security controls.

Overall, threat modeling techniques play a crucial role in identifying and mitigating security risks in microservices architectures. By systematically analyzing potential threats and vulnerabilities, organizations can build more secure and resilient microservices applications that withstand evolving cybersecurity threats.

Vulnerability management is a critical aspect of maintaining the security and integrity of microservices architectures. In today's interconnected and rapidly evolving digital landscape, the identification and remediation of vulnerabilities are essential to mitigate potential security risks and protect sensitive data from exploitation by malicious actors. In microservices architectures, where numerous interconnected components interact dynamically, effective vulnerability management strategies are indispensable to ensure the robustness and resilience of the overall system.

One key aspect of vulnerability management in microservices architectures is the continuous monitoring and assessment of system components for potential security vulnerabilities. This involves the use of various vulnerability scanning tools and techniques to identify weaknesses in both the application code and underlying infrastructure. For instance, organizations can utilize command-line tools such as OWASP ZAP (Zed Attack Proxy) to perform automated security scans of their microservices applications, identifying common vulnerabilities such as SQL injection, cross-site scripting (XSS), and insecure deserialization.

plaintextCopy code

Command: zap-cli --url http://example.com --quick-scan --spider --active-scan

Additionally, organizations can leverage container security scanning tools such as Clair or Trivy to analyze Docker images for known vulnerabilities and dependencies with known security issues. These tools scan container images for vulnerable packages and libraries, enabling organizations to identify and address security risks before deploying microservices into production environments.

plaintextCopy code

Command: trivy image <image-name>

Furthermore, vulnerability management strategies in microservices architectures often involve the implementation of robust patch management processes. This includes regularly updating and patching system components, including operating systems, application frameworks, and third-party libraries, to address known security vulnerabilities and mitigate potential risks. Organizations can utilize package management tools like apt, yum, or npm to update software packages and libraries across their microservices ecosystem.

plaintextCopy code

Command: apt update && apt upgrade

In addition to proactive vulnerability scanning and patch management, organizations can enhance their vulnerability management practices by implementing robust access control mechanisms and least privilege principles within their microservices architectures. This involves restricting access to sensitive resources and data, enforcing strong authentication and authorization mechanisms, and implementing role-based access control (RBAC) policies to limit the privileges of individual microservices and users within the system.

plaintextCopy code

Command: kubectl apply -f rbac-policy.yaml

Moreover, vulnerability management in microservices architectures requires organizations to establish clear incident response procedures and protocols to address security incidents and breaches promptly. This includes defining escalation paths, incident notification procedures, and remediation workflows to ensure swift and effective response to security incidents. By integrating security incident response processes with existing DevOps pipelines, organizations can streamline the detection, investigation, and resolution of security incidents in microservices environments.

Additionally, organizations can leverage threat intelligence feeds and security information and event management (SIEM) systems to enhance their vulnerability management practices in microservices architectures. By continuously monitoring for emerging threats and indicators of compromise, organizations can proactively identify and address potential security vulnerabilities before they can be exploited by attackers. SIEM platforms such as Splunk or ELK Stack enable organizations to aggregate and analyze security event data from across their microservices ecosystem, providing actionable insights into potential security threats and vulnerabilities.

plaintextCopy code

```
Command: splunk search "index=security sourcetype=access_* | stats count by host"
```

Furthermore, vulnerability management strategies in microservices architectures should include regular security assessments and penetration testing to validate the effectiveness of existing security controls and identify potential blind spots or gaps in security posture. By conducting regular security assessments and penetration tests, organizations can proactively identify and address vulnerabilities in their microservices architectures before they can be exploited by attackers.

Overall, effective vulnerability management is essential to maintaining the security and resilience of microservices architectures in today's dynamic and evolving threat landscape. By implementing proactive vulnerability scanning, patch management, access control, incident response, threat intelligence, and security assessments, organizations can mitigate potential security risks and protect their microservices applications and data from exploitation by malicious actors.

Chapter 9: Scalable Authentication and Authorization Solutions for Microservices

Scalable authentication is a fundamental aspect of modern software systems, particularly in distributed environments like microservices architectures. OAuth2 and OpenID Connect (OIDC) have emerged as widely adopted standards for implementing scalable and secure authentication mechanisms in such environments. OAuth2 is an authorization framework that enables third-party applications to access a user's data without exposing their credentials, while OpenID Connect builds on top of OAuth2 to provide authentication capabilities, enabling clients to verify the identity of users based on tokens issued by an identity provider.

OAuth2 and OpenID Connect offer several benefits for implementing scalable authentication in microservices architectures. One key advantage is their support for decentralized authentication and authorization, allowing microservices to offload authentication and authorization responsibilities to specialized identity providers, such as OAuth2 authorization servers or OpenID Connect providers. This decentralized approach enables microservices to focus on their core functionality while leveraging external identity providers for authentication and authorization tasks.

To deploy OAuth2 and OpenID Connect in a microservices architecture, organizations can leverage existing identity providers or deploy their own OAuth2 authorization servers and OpenID Connect providers using open-source solutions such as Keycloak or IdentityServer. These identity providers offer robust features for managing user identities, issuing access tokens, and validating tokens presented by clients, making them ideal for implementing scalable authentication in microservices architectures.

plaintextCopy code

Command: docker run -p 8080:8080 jboss/keycloak

Once deployed, microservices can integrate with the OAuth2 authorization server or OpenID Connect provider using standard protocols and libraries available in various programming languages. For instance, libraries such as Spring Security for Java or IdentityModel for .NET provide comprehensive support for integrating microservices with OAuth2 and OpenID Connect, enabling seamless authentication and authorization flows within the microservices ecosystem.

plaintextCopy code

Command: npm install openid-client

OAuth2 and OpenID Connect also support token-based authentication, wherein clients obtain access tokens or ID tokens from the authorization server or identity provider and present them to microservices to access protected resources. These tokens contain information about the user's identity and permissions, enabling microservices to make access control decisions based on the claims contained within the tokens. By leveraging token-based authentication, microservices can achieve stateless authentication, enabling them to scale horizontally without the need for maintaining session state.

Furthermore, OAuth2 and OpenID Connect offer robust support for various authentication flows, including authorization code flow, implicit flow, and client credentials flow, allowing microservices to choose the most suitable authentication mechanism based on their requirements and security considerations. For instance, the authorization code flow is commonly used for web applications, while the client credentials flow is suitable for machine-to-machine communication between microservices.

In addition to authentication, OAuth2 and OpenID Connect also provide support for fine-grained authorization, enabling microservices to enforce access control policies based on the user's roles, permissions, or other attributes contained within the tokens. This allows organizations to implement flexible and scalable authorization mechanisms within their microservices architectures, ensuring that only authorized users or clients can access protected resources.

Moreover, OAuth2 and OpenID Connect support interoperability and integration with existing identity management systems and standards, enabling organizations to leverage their existing investments in identity infrastructure while adopting modern authentication and authorization mechanisms. This interoperability allows microservices to integrate seamlessly with external identity providers, legacy systems, and third-party applications, ensuring a smooth transition to a microservices-based architecture.

In summary, OAuth2 and OpenID Connect offer powerful capabilities for implementing scalable and secure authentication in microservices architectures. By leveraging decentralized authentication, token-based authentication, fine-grained authorization, and interoperability features provided by OAuth2 and OpenID Connect, organizations can build robust and scalable authentication solutions that meet the demands of modern distributed systems.

Authorization strategies play a critical role in ensuring the security and integrity of large-scale microservices systems. As organizations transition to microservices architectures, they face unique challenges in managing access control across a distributed and dynamic environment. In such systems, traditional monolithic approaches to authorization, such as role-based access control (RBAC), may not suffice due to the complexity and scale of microservices interactions. Therefore, organizations must adopt advanced authorization strategies tailored to the specific characteristics of microservices architectures.

One of the key challenges in large-scale microservices systems is the need for granular and fine-grained access control, where different users or components require varying levels of access to resources. Unlike monolithic applications, where access control is typically managed at the application level, microservices architectures require a decentralized approach to authorization, wherein each microservice is responsible for enforcing access control policies for its resources independently. This decentralized model of authorization allows microservices to scale independently and maintain autonomy over their access control decisions.

To address the challenges of authorization in large-scale microservices systems, organizations can adopt several advanced strategies and techniques. One such strategy is attribute-based access control (ABAC), which enables organizations to define access control policies based on attributes such as user roles, attributes, and environmental factors. ABAC provides a flexible and dynamic approach to authorization, allowing organizations to define complex access control rules that adapt to changing business requirements and user contexts.

Deploying ABAC in a microservices architecture involves defining a centralized policy decision point (PDP) that evaluates access control requests based on predefined policies and attributes. Organizations can use open-source solutions such as OPA (Open Policy Agent) or commercial products like Axiomatics to implement a centralized PDP that orchestrates access control decisions across microservices. The PDP evaluates incoming requests against the defined policies and attributes and makes authorization decisions based on the outcome of the evaluation.

plaintextCopy code

```
Command: docker run -d --name opa-server -p
8181:8181 openpolicyagent/opa run --server
```

Another advanced authorization strategy for large-scale microservices systems is dynamic authorization, which involves dynamically adjusting access control policies based on contextual factors such as user behavior, resource availability, and environmental conditions. Dynamic authorization allows organizations to enforce adaptive access control policies that respond to real-time changes in the system and user behavior, enhancing security and reducing the risk of unauthorized access.

Implementing dynamic authorization in a microservices architecture requires integrating real-time monitoring and analytics capabilities into the authorization pipeline. Organizations can leverage tools such as Prometheus and Grafana to collect and analyze telemetry data from microservices deployments, including user activity, resource utilization, and access patterns. By correlating this data with predefined access control policies, organizations can dynamically adjust authorization decisions in response to emerging threats or anomalies.

plaintextCopy code

Command: kubectl apply -f https://raw.githubusercontent.com/kubernetes/kops/main/addons/monitoring-standalone/v1.0.1.yaml

Additionally, organizations can implement context-based access control, where access control decisions are based on contextual information such as user location, device type, and time of access. Context-based access control enhances security by tailoring access control decisions to the specific context of the user or request, reducing the risk of unauthorized access or data breaches.

Deploying context-based access control in a microservices architecture involves integrating context-awareness capabilities into the authorization pipeline. Organizations can use tools such as Istio or Envoy Proxy to capture contextual information from incoming requests and pass this information to the authorization layer for evaluation. By enriching access control decisions with contextual data, organizations can implement more granular and adaptive access control policies that align with the specific requirements of their microservices environments.

plaintextCopy code

```
Command: istioctl install --set profile=default
```

Furthermore, organizations can leverage identity federation and single sign-on (SSO) solutions to streamline the authentication and authorization process across microservices deployments. Identity federation allows organizations to establish trust relationships with external identity providers, enabling users to authenticate once and access multiple microservices seamlessly. By federating identities across microservices deployments, organizations can centralize access control management and enforce consistent security policies across their entire ecosystem.

In summary, authorization strategies for large-scale microservices systems must be flexible, scalable, and adaptive to meet the unique challenges posed by distributed and dynamic environments. By adopting advanced techniques such as attribute-based access control, dynamic authorization, context-based access control, and identity federation, organizations can implement robust and scalable authorization solutions that enhance security, compliance, and user experience across their microservices architectures.

Chapter 10: Microservices Compliance and Governance Frameworks

Compliance requirements for microservices are critical considerations that organizations must address to ensure regulatory adherence and data protection across their distributed architectures. In an increasingly regulated landscape, where data privacy and security are paramount, meeting compliance standards is not only a legal obligation but also essential for maintaining trust with customers and stakeholders. As organizations embrace microservices architectures to drive agility and scalability, they must navigate a complex regulatory landscape and implement robust compliance frameworks tailored to their specific industry and jurisdictional requirements.

One of the primary compliance considerations for microservices is data privacy regulations, such as the General Data Protection Regulation (GDPR) in the European Union and the California Consumer Privacy Act (CCPA) in the United States. These regulations impose strict requirements on how organizations collect, store, and process personal data, including customer information and sensitive financial data. To comply with these regulations, organizations must implement data protection measures, such as encryption, pseudonymization, and access controls, to safeguard sensitive data across their microservices ecosystem.

Deploying encryption in a microservices architecture involves encrypting data at rest and in transit to protect it from unauthorized access or disclosure. Organizations can use encryption libraries such as OpenSSL or cryptographic tools like HashiCorp Vault to implement encryption mechanisms within their microservices deployments. By encrypting sensitive data stored in databases or transmitted between microservices, organizations can mitigate the risk of data breaches and ensure compliance with data privacy regulations.

plaintextCopy code

Command: openssl enc -aes-256-cbc -salt -in plaintext.txt -out encrypted.txt

Another critical compliance consideration for microservices is regulatory reporting and auditability. Many industries, including finance, healthcare, and government, are subject to strict regulatory requirements that mandate regular audits and reporting to demonstrate compliance with industry standards and regulations. In a microservices environment, where systems are distributed across multiple services and infrastructure components, maintaining visibility and accountability for compliance can be challenging.

Implementing logging and auditing mechanisms is essential for maintaining compliance in a microservices architecture. Organizations can use logging frameworks such as Log4j or centralized logging platforms like ELK Stack (Elasticsearch, Logstash, Kibana) to capture and store log data from microservices deployments. By aggregating and analyzing log data, organizations can track user activity, system events, and security incidents to ensure compliance with regulatory requirements and facilitate audit trails.

plaintextCopy code

Command: kubectl apply -f https://download.elastic.co/downloads/eck/1.5.0/all-in-one.yaml

Furthermore, regulatory compliance often requires organizations to implement access controls and identity management mechanisms to restrict access to sensitive resources and data. Role-based access control (RBAC) is a common approach to access control in microservices architectures, where users are assigned roles and permissions that dictate their level of access to system resources. Organizations can use identity and access management (IAM) platforms such as Keycloak or Okta to manage user identities and enforce access control policies across their microservices deployments.

plaintextCopy code

Command: helm repo add codecentric https://codecentric.github.io/helm-charts

Moreover, compliance requirements may necessitate organizations to implement data retention and deletion policies to manage the lifecycle of data stored within their microservices ecosystem. Data retention policies specify how long data should be retained before it is deleted or archived, while data deletion policies ensure that data is securely erased from storage systems once it is no longer needed. Organizations can use data management platforms such as Apache Kafka or Apache

NiFi to implement data lifecycle management policies and automate data retention and deletion processes.
plaintextCopy code

Command: kubectl apply -f https://github.com/apache/nifi-kubernetes-operator/releases/download/v1.13.1/nifi-operator.crds.yaml

Additionally, compliance with industry-specific regulations, such as the Health Insurance Portability and Accountability Act (HIPAA) in healthcare or the Payment Card Industry Data Security Standard (PCI DSS) in the financial sector, requires organizations to implement additional security controls and safeguards to protect sensitive data and ensure regulatory compliance. These regulations may mandate the use of specific encryption algorithms, authentication mechanisms, and security protocols to safeguard data and prevent unauthorized access or disclosure.

In summary, compliance requirements for microservices encompass a wide range of considerations, including data privacy, auditability, access control, and data lifecycle management. By implementing robust compliance frameworks tailored to their specific industry and regulatory requirements, organizations can ensure regulatory adherence, mitigate risk, and build trust with customers and stakeholders. As microservices architectures continue to evolve, organizations must remain vigilant and proactive in addressing compliance challenges to maintain the integrity and security of their systems.

Implementing governance frameworks for microservices compliance is essential for ensuring that organizations adhere to regulatory requirements, industry standards, and internal policies across their distributed architectures. Governance frameworks provide guidelines, processes, and controls to manage and enforce compliance, mitigate risks, and ensure consistency and accountability in microservices development and operations. These frameworks encompass a range of practices, including policy definition, enforcement mechanisms, monitoring, and reporting, to address the complexities of compliance in dynamic and decentralized environments.

One of the key aspects of implementing governance frameworks for microservices compliance is establishing clear policies and standards that govern the development, deployment, and operation of microservices. These policies define requirements related to data privacy, security, availability, performance, and other compliance considerations. For example, organizations may define policies specifying the encryption requirements for sensitive data, access control measures, authentication mechanisms, and data retention policies to ensure compliance with regulatory requirements such as GDPR, HIPAA, or PCI DSS.

plaintextCopy code

```
Command: kubectl apply -f policy.yaml
```

Once policies are defined, organizations need to establish mechanisms for enforcing compliance throughout the microservices lifecycle. This involves integrating compliance checks and controls into the development, deployment, and monitoring processes to ensure that microservices adhere to established policies and standards. Tools such as Kubernetes admission controllers or policy enforcement frameworks like Open Policy Agent (OPA) can be used to enforce compliance rules and policies at various stages of the microservices lifecycle.

plaintextCopy code

Command: kubectl apply -f opa-policy.yaml

In addition to policy enforcement, organizations must implement monitoring and auditing mechanisms to assess compliance and identify potential violations or deviations from established policies. This involves collecting and analyzing data from microservices deployments, infrastructure components, and user activities to detect anomalies, security incidents, or non-compliant behavior. Monitoring tools such as Prometheus, Grafana, or commercial solutions like Datadog or Splunk can provide real-time visibility into the performance, security, and compliance posture of microservices environments.

plaintextCopy code

Command: helm install prometheus stable/prometheus

Moreover, governance frameworks for microservices compliance often include mechanisms for risk management and remediation. This involves identifying and assessing risks associated with non-compliance, prioritizing remediation efforts based on risk severity, and implementing controls to mitigate identified risks. Organizations can use risk assessment frameworks such as the NIST Cybersecurity Framework or ISO 27001 to identify and prioritize risks and implement risk mitigation measures tailored to their specific compliance requirements.

plaintextCopy code

Command: kubectl apply -f nist-framework.yaml

Furthermore, governance frameworks may include provisions for documentation and reporting to demonstrate compliance with regulatory requirements and internal policies. This involves maintaining comprehensive documentation of policies, procedures, and controls, as well as generating audit reports and compliance attestations to provide evidence of compliance to regulators, auditors, and stakeholders. Documentation tools such as Confluence or Wiki pages can be used to create and maintain compliance documentation, while reporting tools such as Elasticsearch and Kibana can generate compliance reports and dashboards.

plaintextCopy code

Command: helm install elasticsearch elastic/elasticsearch

Additionally, governance frameworks should incorporate mechanisms for continuous improvement and adaptation to evolving compliance requirements and industry best practices. This involves regularly reviewing and updating policies and controls based on changes in regulations, emerging threats, and lessons learned from security incidents or compliance audits. Organizations can establish governance committees or compliance teams responsible for monitoring regulatory changes, assessing their impact on microservices compliance, and updating governance frameworks accordingly.

In summary, implementing governance frameworks for microservices compliance is essential for ensuring that organizations meet regulatory requirements, mitigate risks, and maintain the integrity and security of their microservices environments. By establishing clear policies, enforcing compliance controls, monitoring adherence, and continuously improving governance practices, organizations can build trust with customers, regulators, and stakeholders and demonstrate their commitment to compliance and security in an increasingly regulated digital landscape.

BOOK 4
MICROSERVICES MASTERY
EXPERT INSIGHTS INTO DEPLOYMENT, MONITORING,
AND MAINTENANCE

ROB BOTWRIGHT

Chapter 1: Canary Releases and Blue-Green Deployments

Canary releases, an incremental rollout technique for deploying software updates, serve as a risk mitigation strategy by allowing organizations to test new features or changes in a controlled manner before making them available to all users. The concept of canary releases originates from the practice of using canaries in coal mines to detect toxic gases; similarly, in software development, canary releases involve deploying changes to a small subset of users or infrastructure to detect and mitigate potential issues before full deployment. This approach minimizes the impact of bugs or performance issues by limiting exposure to a small audience initially, allowing organizations to gather feedback, monitor system health, and gradually increase the rollout if no issues are detected.

To implement canary releases, organizations typically utilize deployment automation tools and container orchestration platforms such as Kubernetes. These platforms enable organizations to define deployment strategies that specify how updates should be rolled out, including canary deployments. In a canary deployment, a small percentage of the production traffic is redirected to the new version of the software while the majority of the traffic continues to be served by the stable version. This allows organizations to

observe the behavior of the new version in a real-world environment and assess its performance and reliability.
plaintextCopy code

Command: kubectl apply -f canary-deployment.yaml

One common technique used in canary releases is traffic splitting, where organizations configure load balancers or service meshes to distribute traffic between different versions of a service based on predefined criteria such as HTTP headers, user identities, or geographic location. By gradually increasing the proportion of traffic routed to the new version, organizations can monitor key metrics such as error rates, latency, and user engagement to determine if the new version meets performance and reliability targets.

plaintextCopy code

Command: kubectl apply -f traffic-splitting.yaml

Another important aspect of canary releases is monitoring and observability. Organizations need to instrument their applications and infrastructure to collect metrics, logs, and traces that provide insight into the behavior and performance of the new version during the canary deployment. Monitoring tools such as Prometheus, Grafana, and Jaeger can be used to visualize key metrics and identify any anomalies or regressions that may occur during the rollout.

plaintextCopy code

Command: helm install prometheus stable/prometheus

Additionally, organizations can implement automated testing and validation techniques to ensure that the new version meets functional and non-functional requirements before and during the canary deployment. This may include unit tests, integration tests, and end-to-end tests that validate the behavior of the application under various conditions. Continuous integration and continuous deployment (CI/CD) pipelines play a crucial role in automating the testing and deployment process, enabling organizations to rapidly iterate and deliver updates with confidence.

plaintextCopy code

Command: git push origin feature-branch

One of the key benefits of canary releases is their ability to detect and mitigate issues early in the deployment process, thereby reducing the risk of widespread outages or service disruptions. By limiting the blast radius of changes, organizations can minimize the impact on users and quickly roll back to the previous version if issues are detected. This iterative approach to deployment fosters a culture of experimentation and continuous improvement, allowing organizations to innovate rapidly while maintaining high levels of reliability and stability.

In summary, canary releases offer a powerful technique for managing risk and ensuring the smooth rollout of software updates in modern distributed systems. By incrementally exposing new versions of software to a subset of users or infrastructure, organizations can gather feedback, monitor performance, and validate changes before fully committing to deployment. When combined with robust monitoring, automated testing, and deployment automation practices, canary releases enable organizations to deliver high-quality software with confidence, even in complex and dynamic environments.

Blue-green deployments are a deployment strategy used in software development to achieve zero-downtime deployments by minimizing or eliminating disruptions to user-facing services during updates or releases. This approach involves maintaining two identical production environments: one active (blue) and the other inactive (green). When deploying updates or changes, traffic is gradually shifted from the active environment to the new environment, allowing organizations to verify the new version's stability and functionality before directing all traffic to it.

To implement blue-green deployments, organizations typically utilize deployment automation tools and infrastructure orchestration platforms such as Kubernetes. These platforms allow organizations to define deployment strategies and automate the process of provisioning and managing infrastructure resources. With Kubernetes, for example, blue-green deployments can be achieved using deployment objects and service objects to manage the rollout of new versions.

plaintextCopy code

Command: kubectl apply -f blue-green-deployment.yaml

In a blue-green deployment, the active environment (blue) serves production traffic while the inactive environment (green) remains idle. Once the new version of the application is deployed to the green environment and validated, traffic can be gradually shifted from the blue environment to the green environment using techniques such as load balancer configuration or DNS updates.

plaintextCopy code

Command: kubectl scale deployment blue-replica-set --replicas=0 Command: kubectl scale deployment green-replica-set --replicas=3

One common approach to shifting traffic in a blue-green deployment is to update the configuration of a load balancer to route traffic to the new environment. For example, if using Kubernetes, organizations can update the service object associated with the application to point to the pods in the green environment.

plaintextCopy code

Command: kubectl apply -f service-blue-to-green.yaml

Alternatively, organizations can use DNS-based techniques to direct traffic to the new environment. This involves updating the DNS records associated with the application domain to point to the IP addresses or endpoints of the green environment.

plaintextCopy code

Command: kubectl apply -f update-dns-record.yaml

Once traffic has been successfully shifted to the green environment and the new version has been validated, organizations can decommission the blue environment and make the green environment the new active environment. This completes the blue-green deployment process and ensures that users are seamlessly transitioned to the updated version of the application without experiencing any downtime or disruptions.

plaintextCopy code

Command: kubectl delete deployment blue-replica-set

One of the key benefits of blue-green deployments is their ability to minimize risk and ensure the reliability of software updates by providing a controlled and reversible deployment process. By maintaining two separate environments and gradually transitioning traffic between them, organizations can verify the new version's stability and functionality before fully committing to deployment.

Additionally, blue-green deployments enable organizations to roll back changes quickly and easily in the event of issues or regressions. If problems are detected during the deployment process, organizations can simply redirect traffic back to the blue environment while they address the issues in the green environment, ensuring minimal impact on users.

Overall, blue-green deployments offer a robust and reliable deployment strategy for organizations seeking to achieve zero-downtime deployments and maintain high levels of availability and reliability for their applications. When combined with automation, monitoring, and testing practices, blue-green deployments empower organizations to deliver software updates with confidence, enabling rapid innovation and iteration while minimizing risk and disruption to users.

Chapter 2: Infrastructure as Code (IaC) for Microservices

Infrastructure as Code (IaC) is a methodology used in software development and IT operations to automate the provisioning and management of infrastructure resources through machine-readable configuration files or scripts. It enables organizations to define and manage their infrastructure using code, treating infrastructure as software artifacts that can be version-controlled, tested, and deployed alongside application code. By adopting IaC practices, organizations can achieve greater consistency, scalability, and efficiency in managing their infrastructure, leading to improved agility, reliability, and cost-effectiveness.

One of the key principles of IaC is to define infrastructure resources and configurations using declarative or imperative syntax, allowing developers and operators to specify desired states rather than manual steps to provision or configure resources. This approach enables infrastructure to be provisioned and managed programmatically, reducing the risk of human error and ensuring consistency across environments.

In practice, IaC is often implemented using configuration management tools such as Terraform, Ansible, or Chef, which provide abstractions and tooling to define, provision, and manage infrastructure resources. These tools support a wide range of cloud providers, virtualization platforms, and other infrastructure technologies, allowing organizations to manage diverse and complex environments using a unified and standardized approach.

plaintextCopy code

Command: terraform apply -auto-approve

Terraform, for example, uses a declarative configuration language called HashiCorp Configuration Language (HCL) to define infrastructure resources and their dependencies. Developers can write Terraform configuration files (typically with a .tf extension) that describe the desired state of infrastructure resources, such as virtual machines, networks, storage, and security groups.

hclCopy code

```
# Example Terraform configuration for provisioning an AWS EC2 instance resource "aws_instance" "example" {
ami = "ami-0c55b159cbfafe1f0" instance_type = "t2.micro" tags = { Name = "example-instance" } }
```

Once the configuration files are defined, developers can use the Terraform CLI to apply the configuration and provision the specified resources. Terraform will automatically create, update, or delete resources as needed to ensure that the current state matches the desired state defined in the configuration files.

Another popular tool for implementing IaC is Ansible, an open-source automation platform that uses a declarative YAML syntax to define infrastructure configurations and automation tasks. Ansible playbooks allow developers to define a series of tasks to be executed on remote hosts, enabling infrastructure provisioning, configuration management, and application deployment.

plaintextCopy code

Command: ansible-playbook -i inventory playbook.yaml

Ansible playbooks are typically organized into tasks, which represent individual actions to be performed, and roles, which encapsulate sets of tasks and can be reused across multiple playbooks. This modular approach allows developers to manage complex infrastructure configurations and automation workflows with ease.

yamlCopy code

```
# Example Ansible playbook for provisioning an NGINX web server - hosts: web_servers tasks: - name: Install NGINX package yum: name: nginx state: present - name: Configure NGINX service systemd: name: nginx enabled: yes state: started
```

By defining infrastructure configurations and automation tasks in code, organizations can leverage software development best practices such as version control, testing, and code review to ensure the reliability and repeatability of their infrastructure deployments. This enables teams to collaborate more effectively, track changes to infrastructure configurations over time, and rollback changes when necessary.

Furthermore, IaC enables organizations to adopt agile and DevOps practices by integrating infrastructure provisioning and management into continuous integration and continuous delivery (CI/CD) pipelines. By automating the deployment of infrastructure alongside application code, organizations can accelerate the delivery of new features and updates while maintaining consistency and reliability across environments.

In summary, Infrastructure as Code (IaC) is a powerful methodology for automating the provisioning and management of infrastructure resources using machine-readable configuration files or scripts. By treating infrastructure as code and adopting IaC practices, organizations can achieve greater consistency, scalability, and efficiency in managing their infrastructure, leading to improved agility, reliability, and cost-effectiveness.

Implementing Infrastructure as Code (IaC) with tools like Terraform and AWS CloudFormation is crucial for modern software development and operations teams seeking to automate the provisioning and management of cloud infrastructure resources. These tools enable organizations to define their infrastructure requirements in code, allowing for reproducible, scalable, and consistent deployments across various cloud environments.

Terraform is an open-source IaC tool developed by HashiCorp, designed to manage infrastructure resources across multiple cloud providers and on-premises environments. With Terraform, infrastructure configurations are defined using a declarative language called HashiCorp Configuration Language (HCL), allowing users to specify the desired state of their infrastructure in code. This code is then used to create an execution plan that describes the actions Terraform will take to achieve the desired state, such as provisioning or updating resources.

plaintextCopy code

Command: terraform init

The first step in using Terraform is to initialize the working directory with the **terraform init** command. This command initializes the Terraform environment, downloading any necessary plugins and modules required for the configuration.

plaintextCopy code

Command: terraform plan

Next, users can use the **terraform plan** command to generate an execution plan based on the defined configuration. This plan provides a preview of the actions Terraform will take to achieve the desired state, including creating, updating, or deleting resources.

plaintextCopy code

Command: terraform apply

Once satisfied with the execution plan, users can apply the changes to their infrastructure using the **terraform apply** command. Terraform will then execute the plan, provisioning or updating resources as necessary to reach the desired state.

hclCopy code

```
# Example Terraform configuration for provisioning an AWS EC2 instance resource "aws_instance" "example" {
ami = "ami-0c55b159cbfafe1f0" instance_type = "t2.micro" tags = { Name = "example-instance" } }
```

In this example, the Terraform configuration defines an AWS EC2 instance using the **aws_instance** resource type. The configuration specifies the Amazon Machine Image (AMI), instance type, and tags for the EC2 instance.

AWS CloudFormation is a native IaC service provided by Amazon Web Services (AWS) that enables users to define and manage AWS infrastructure resources using JSON or YAML templates. CloudFormation templates allow users to describe their infrastructure requirements and dependencies in a declarative format, similar to Terraform.

plaintextCopy code

Command: aws cloudformation create-stack

To deploy a CloudFormation template, users can use the **aws cloudformation create-stack** command, specifying the template file and any required parameters. CloudFormation will then create the stack and provision the specified resources according to the template.

plaintextCopy code

Command: aws cloudformation update-stack

If changes need to be made to an existing stack, users can use the **aws cloudformation update-stack** command to update the stack with the changes specified in the updated template.

yamlCopy code

Example CloudFormation template for provisioning an S3 bucket Resources: MyS3Bucket: Type: AWS::S3::Bucket Properties: BucketName: my-bucket

In this example, the CloudFormation template defines an S3 bucket resource using the **AWS::S3::Bucket** resource type. The template specifies the bucket name as "my-bucket".

Both Terraform and AWS CloudFormation offer powerful features for managing infrastructure as code, allowing users to automate the deployment and management of cloud resources with ease. While Terraform provides cross-cloud compatibility and a rich ecosystem of plugins and modules, CloudFormation offers seamless integration with AWS services and native support for AWS resource types. Organizations can choose the tool that best fits their requirements and workflows to implement IaC effectively and efficiently.

Chapter 3: Microservices Deployment Orchestration with Helm Charts

Helm is a package manager for Kubernetes applications that streamlines the installation and management of Kubernetes resources using pre-configured templates called Helm charts. Helm charts provide a convenient and reusable way to define, package, and deploy complex Kubernetes applications, making it easier for developers and operators to manage their containerized workloads.

With Helm, users can define their application's structure, dependencies, and configurations using simple YAML files, encapsulating all the necessary Kubernetes resources into a single package. This package, known as a Helm chart, can then be easily shared, versioned, and deployed across different Kubernetes clusters.

plaintextCopy code

Command: helm create <chart-name>

To create a new Helm chart, users can use the **helm create** command followed by the desired chart name. This command generates the basic directory structure and template files required for the chart, including the Chart.yaml file, values.yaml file, and templates directory.

The Chart.yaml file contains metadata about the chart, such as its name, version, and description, while the values.yaml file defines default configuration values that can be overridden during installation. The templates directory contains Kubernetes manifest files written in YAML or Go template format, defining the resources to be deployed.

yamlCopy code

Example Chart.yaml file for a Helm chart apiVersion: v2 name: my-chart version: 0.1.0 description: A Helm chart for deploying a sample application

In this example, the Chart.yaml file specifies metadata for a Helm chart named "my-chart" with version 0.1.0 and a brief description of the chart.

yamlCopy code

Example values.yaml file for a Helm chart replicaCount: 1 image: repository: nginx tag: latest

The values.yaml file defines default configuration values for the Helm chart, such as the number of replica pods and the container image repository and tag.

yamlCopy code

Example deployment.yaml template file for a Helm chart apiVersion: apps/v1 kind: Deployment metadata: name: {{ include "my-chart.fullname" . }} spec: replicas: {{ .Values.replicaCount }} selector: matchLabels: app: {{ include "my-chart.name" . }} template: metadata: labels: app: {{ include "my-chart.name" . }} spec: containers: - name: {{ .Chart.Name }} image: "{{ .Values.image.repository }}:{{ .Values.image.tag }}" ports: - containerPort: 80

In this example, the deployment.yaml template file defines a Kubernetes Deployment resource using Go template syntax. The template uses values defined in the values.yaml file, such as the replica count and container image repository, to generate the Deployment manifest.

plaintextCopy code

Command: helm install <release-name> <chart-name>

Once the Helm chart is defined, users can install it onto a Kubernetes cluster using the **helm install** command followed by the desired release name and chart name. Helm will then render the templates, generate the corresponding Kubernetes manifests, and deploy the resources onto the cluster.

plaintextCopy code

Command: helm upgrade <release-name> <chart-name>

To update an existing Helm release with changes made to the chart or its configuration values, users can use the **helm upgrade** command followed by the release name and chart name. Helm will apply the updates to the release, ensuring that the deployed resources reflect the latest changes.

Helm charts simplify the process of deploying and managing Kubernetes applications by providing a standardized and reusable packaging format. With Helm, users can easily share, version, and deploy their applications across different Kubernetes environments, streamlining the development and operations workflow for containerized workloads.

Helm charts provide a powerful mechanism for defining, packaging, and deploying Kubernetes applications, but their true flexibility lies in the ability to customize and template the configuration to suit specific use cases and environments. In this section, we will explore advanced techniques for customizing Helm charts, including parameterization, conditionals, loops, and functions.

Parameterization is a fundamental concept in Helm chart customization, allowing users to define configurable values that can be overridden during installation. By parameterizing values in the values.yaml file, users can create reusable charts that adapt to different deployment scenarios without modifying the underlying templates.

plaintextCopy code

```
Command: helm install <release-name> <chart-name> --set key1=value1,key2=value2
```

During installation, users can override default values defined in the values.yaml file by passing custom values via the **--set** flag. This allows for on-the-fly configuration adjustments without modifying the chart itself, making it easy to tailor deployments to specific requirements.

Conditional logic enables users to define different paths or configurations based on specific conditions, such as the presence of a certain value or the environment type. Helm provides several conditional functions, such as **if**, **eq**, **ne**, **and**, and **or**, which can be used to control the flow of template execution.

yamlCopy code

```
{{ if .Values.enableFeature }} apiVersion: v1 kind: Service metadata: name: my-service spec: selector: app: my-app ports: - protocol: TCP port: 80 {{ end }}
```

In this example, the Service resource will only be rendered if the **enableFeature** value is set to true in the values.yaml file, allowing for dynamic inclusion or exclusion of resources based on configuration settings.

Loops provide a mechanism for iterating over lists or maps and generating multiple instances of a template based on each item in the collection. Helm supports the **range** function, which can be used to iterate over arrays, slices, or maps and execute template blocks for each element.

yamlCopy code

```
{{ range .Values.backendServices }} apiVersion: v1 kind: Service metadata: name: {{ .name }} spec: selector: app: {{ .name }} ports: - protocol: TCP port: {{ .port }} {{ end }}
```

In this example, the range function iterates over the **backendServices** list defined in the values.yaml file and generates a Service resource for each item in the list, allowing for the dynamic creation of multiple resources based on configuration data.

Functions provide a way to perform computations, transformations, or operations within Helm templates, enabling advanced logic and data manipulation. Helm includes a variety of built-in functions, such as **tpl**, **toYaml**, **toJson**, **printf**, and **include**, which can be used to achieve complex templating tasks.

yamlCopy code

```
{{ $serviceName := include "my-chart.fullname" . }} apiVersion: v1 kind: Service metadata: name: {{ $serviceName }} spec: selector: app: {{ $serviceName }} ports: - protocol: TCP port: 80
```

In this example, the **include** function is used to dynamically generate a unique service name based on the release name and namespace, ensuring that each deployment gets its own distinct service identifier.

By mastering these advanced customization and templating techniques, users can create Helm charts that are highly flexible, reusable, and adaptable to a wide range of deployment scenarios. Whether it's parameterizing values, incorporating conditional logic, iterating over collections, or leveraging functions, Helm provides a powerful toolkit for crafting sophisticated Kubernetes application deployments.

Chapter 4: Implementing Service Mesh for Microservices Communication and Observability

Service Mesh Architecture refers to a pattern used to manage service-to-service communication within complex distributed systems. In this architecture, a dedicated infrastructure layer is added to handle communication between microservices, often referred to as the "data plane." The data plane typically consists of lightweight proxies deployed alongside each service instance, allowing for transparent interception and control of network traffic. These proxies facilitate various functionalities such as service discovery, load balancing, encryption, authentication, authorization, and observability.

One of the key components of a service mesh architecture is the proxy, which acts as an intermediary between services. The most commonly used proxies in service mesh architectures are Envoy, Linkerd, and Istio's Envoy-based sidecar proxy. These proxies intercept all incoming and outgoing traffic to and from the service instances, allowing for centralized control and management of communication.

bashCopy code

Command: istioctl install --set profile=default

For example, in Istio, the **istioctl install** command installs the Istio control plane components, including the Envoy proxy, into the Kubernetes cluster. Users can customize the installation by setting various parameters, such as the profile type.

Service discovery is another critical aspect of service mesh architecture, enabling services to locate and communicate with each other dynamically. Rather than relying on static configurations or DNS-based discovery, service mesh architectures often use a service registry, such as Consul, etcd, or Kubernetes' built-in service discovery mechanism. These registries maintain up-to-date information about the available services and their network locations, allowing proxies to route traffic accordingly.

bashCopy code

Command: kubectl get services

For instance, Kubernetes users can use the **kubectl get services** command to retrieve information about the services running in the cluster, including their IP addresses and port numbers.

Load balancing is another essential feature provided by service mesh architectures, ensuring that traffic is distributed evenly across multiple instances of a service. Proxies within the service mesh can perform intelligent load balancing algorithms based on factors such as server health, latency, and request rates, improving overall system reliability and performance.

yamlCopy code

apiVersion: networking.istio.io/v1alpha3 kind: VirtualService metadata: name: my-service spec: hosts: - my-service http: - route: - destination: host: my-service port: number: 8080

In Istio, users can define virtual services to configure how traffic is routed to different service versions or subsets. This YAML manifest directs traffic destined for **my-service** to the service running on port 8080.

Security is a critical concern in distributed systems, and service mesh architectures offer several features to enhance security. Mutual TLS (mTLS) encryption, for example, can be enforced between service instances, ensuring that all communication is encrypted and authenticated. Additionally, service mesh architectures support fine-grained access control policies, allowing administrators to define who can access specific services and what actions they can perform.

```yaml
yamlCopy code
apiVersion: "security.istio.io/v1beta1" kind: "AuthorizationPolicy" metadata: name: "my-service-policy" spec: selector: matchLabels: app: my-service action: ALLOW rules: - from: - source: notNamespaces: ["default"]
```

In Istio, users can create authorization policies to define access control rules for specific services. This YAML manifest allows traffic from namespaces other than the default namespace to access the **my-service** service.

Observability is another essential aspect of service mesh architectures, providing insights into the behavior and performance of distributed systems. Proxies within the service mesh collect telemetry data such as request latency, error rates, and traffic volumes, which can be aggregated and visualized using monitoring tools like Prometheus, Grafana, and Jaeger.

```bash
bashCopy code
```

Command: kubectl port-forward svc/prometheus-server 9090:80

For example, users can use the **kubectl port-forward** command to forward the Prometheus service port to their local machine, allowing them to access the Prometheus UI at http://localhost:9090 and view metrics collected from the service mesh.

Overall, service mesh architecture offers a robust foundation for building and operating complex distributed systems by providing features such as service discovery, load balancing, security, and observability. By deploying proxies alongside service instances and leveraging centralized control and management, organizations can achieve greater resilience, scalability, and visibility in their microservices environments.

Service mesh technology has gained significant traction in recent years due to its ability to address the challenges associated with managing communication between microservices in distributed systems. Among its key features, traffic management, security, and observability stand out as critical components that contribute to the reliability, security, and performance of microservices architectures.

Traffic management within a service mesh refers to the ability to control and regulate the flow of network traffic between microservices. This feature is crucial for ensuring that requests are properly routed, load is evenly distributed across service instances, and traffic is resilient to failures. Service mesh platforms offer a variety of traffic management capabilities, including service discovery, load balancing, traffic shaping, and routing rules.

bashCopy code

Command: istioctl create -f virtualservice.yaml

For instance, Istio, a popular service mesh implementation, allows users to define traffic routing rules using VirtualService resources. By creating and applying YAML manifests like the one above, users can specify how incoming requests should be routed based on criteria such as HTTP headers, request paths, or source IP addresses.

Security is another critical aspect of service mesh technology, particularly in environments where sensitive data is transmitted between microservices. Service mesh platforms offer a range of security features to encrypt communication, authenticate service identities, and enforce access control policies.

yamlCopy code

apiVersion: security.istio.io/v1beta1 kind: AuthorizationPolicy metadata: name: allow-productpage-only spec: selector: matchLabels: app: productpage action: ALLOW rules: - from: - source: namespaces: ["default"]

In Istio, for example, administrators can define fine-grained access control policies using AuthorizationPolicy resources. The YAML manifest above allows only traffic originating from the "default" namespace to access the "productpage" service.

Observability is essential for gaining insight into the behavior and performance of microservices within a distributed system. Service mesh platforms provide robust observability features that enable real-time monitoring, logging, and tracing of network traffic and service interactions.

bashCopy code

Command: kubectl port-forward svc/grafana 3000:80

For example, Grafana, a popular observability tool, can be deployed alongside Istio to visualize metrics collected from the service mesh. Users can access the Grafana dashboard by forwarding the Grafana service port to their local machine using the **kubectl port-forward** command.

The combination of traffic management, security, and observability features offered by service mesh technology provides organizations with the necessary tools to build and operate reliable, secure, and scalable microservices architectures. By leveraging these features, teams can effectively manage communication between microservices, detect and mitigate security threats, and gain insights into the performance and health of their applications.

Furthermore, service mesh platforms often integrate seamlessly with existing container orchestration systems such as Kubernetes, making it easy to deploy and manage service mesh components alongside microservices deployments.

bashCopy code

Command: istioctl install --set profile=default

For instance, Istio can be installed into a Kubernetes cluster using the **istioctl install** command, with options to customize the installation profile based on specific requirements.

In summary, service mesh technology offers a comprehensive set of features for managing microservices communication, addressing key challenges related to traffic management, security, and observability. By adopting a service mesh approach, organizations can streamline the operation of their microservices architectures and ensure the reliability and security of their applications.

Chapter 5: Distributed Tracing and Log Aggregation for Microservices Monitoring

Distributed tracing is a crucial technique in the realm of microservices and distributed systems, enabling developers and operators to gain visibility into the flow of requests as they traverse across multiple services. At its core, distributed tracing provides insights into the latency, performance bottlenecks, and dependencies between different components within a distributed system. By instrumenting applications with tracing libraries, developers can generate trace data that captures the path of a request as it propagates through various microservices. This trace data typically includes information such as timestamps, service names, and unique identifiers for each span, allowing for the reconstruction of the entire request lifecycle.

bashCopy code

Command: curl -X POST http://localhost:14268/api/traces -H "Content-Type: application/json" -d @trace.json

To deploy distributed tracing in a microservices environment, one common approach is to use an open-source distributed tracing system such as Jaeger or Zipkin. These systems provide components for collecting, storing, and visualizing trace data generated by instrumented applications. For example, Jaeger can be deployed to a Kubernetes cluster using Helm charts, which simplifies the process of setting up the necessary infrastructure.

bashCopy code

Command: helm install jaeger jaegertracing/jaeger

Once deployed, developers can instrument their microservices applications with tracing libraries that integrate with the chosen distributed tracing system. For instance, the OpenTelemetry project offers libraries in various programming languages that can be easily integrated into microservices codebases to generate trace data.

javaCopy code

```
import io.opentelemetry.api.trace.Span; import
io.opentelemetry.api.trace.Tracer; import
io.opentelemetry.api.GlobalOpenTelemetry; import
io.opentelemetry.context.Scope; Tracer tracer =
GlobalOpenTelemetry.getTracer("my-tracer"); Span
span = tracer.spanBuilder("my-
operation").startSpan(); try (Scope scope =
span.makeCurrent()) { // Execute operation } finally {
span.end(); }
```

Once the applications are instrumented and deployed, distributed tracing systems collect trace data emitted by the instrumented services and store it in a centralized data store. This data is then made available for visualization and analysis through a user interface provided by the distributed tracing system.

bashCopy code

Command: kubectl port-forward svc/jaeger-query 16686:16686

For example, Jaeger provides a web-based user interface that allows users to query and visualize trace data in real-time. By forwarding the Jaeger Query service port to a local machine, users can access the Jaeger UI and explore traces generated by their microservices applications.

Distributed tracing offers several benefits in the context of microservices architectures. One of the key advantages is the ability to identify performance bottlenecks and latency issues across distributed systems. By analyzing trace data, developers can pinpoint the specific services or components that contribute to increased response times and optimize them accordingly.

Another benefit of distributed tracing is its role in facilitating root cause analysis and debugging in distributed systems. When an issue arises, developers can trace the path of a request through the system and identify any failures or errors that occur along the way. This visibility into the request lifecycle can significantly reduce the time it takes to diagnose and resolve issues in microservices environments.

Moreover, distributed tracing enables developers to understand the dependencies between different services within a distributed system. By visualizing the flow of requests between services, developers can gain insights into service interactions and dependencies, allowing them to make informed decisions when designing and evolving microservices architectures.

In summary, distributed tracing is a powerful technique for gaining visibility into the behavior and performance of microservices and distributed systems. By instrumenting applications with tracing libraries and deploying distributed tracing systems, developers can monitor and analyze the flow of requests, identify performance bottlenecks, and debug issues more effectively. This visibility is crucial for building and maintaining reliable and performant microservices architectures in modern software development environments.

Log aggregation is a critical aspect of managing and monitoring distributed systems, where applications generate a vast amount of logs across various services and components. To effectively manage this log data, organizations employ log aggregation strategies, leveraging tools like Elasticsearch and Fluentd to centralize, index, and analyze logs from multiple sources. These tools form the backbone of log aggregation pipelines, enabling developers and operators to gain insights into system behavior, diagnose issues, and ensure the reliability and performance of their applications.

```bash
bashCopy code
Command: kubectl apply -f fluentd-config.yaml
```

Deploying a log aggregation solution typically involves setting up and configuring both the log collector and the storage backend. In the case of Elasticsearch and Fluentd, Fluentd serves as the log collector responsible for collecting log data from various sources, transforming it into a structured format, and forwarding it to Elasticsearch for storage and indexing. Kubernetes users can deploy Fluentd as a DaemonSet to ensure that each node in the cluster has a Fluentd agent running to collect logs from local containers.

yamlCopy code

```
# fluentd-config.yaml apiVersion: v1 kind: ConfigMap metadata: name: fluentd-config data: fluent.conf: | <source> @type tail path /var/log/containers/*.log pos_file /var/log/fluentd-containers.log.pos tag kubernetes.* read_from_head true <parse> @type json </parse> </source> <match **> @type elasticsearch hosts elasticsearch.default.svc.cluster.local:9200 logstash_format true logstash_prefix kubernetes logstash_dateformat %Y%m%d include_tag_key true tag_key @log_name flush_interval 5s </match>
```

Once deployed, Fluentd collects logs from containers running on Kubernetes nodes and forwards them to Elasticsearch for indexing and storage. Elasticsearch serves as the backend storage for log data, providing capabilities for indexing, searching, and analyzing logs in real-time. Kubernetes users can deploy Elasticsearch to their cluster using Helm charts, which simplifies the process of setting up and configuring Elasticsearch instances.

bashCopy code

```
Command: helm install elasticsearch elastic/elasticsearch
```

With the log aggregation pipeline in place, organizations can leverage the capabilities of Elasticsearch and

Fluentd to gain insights into their application logs. Elasticsearch provides powerful querying capabilities, allowing users to search and filter logs based on various criteria such as timestamps, log levels, or specific keywords. Users can also create dashboards and visualizations using tools like Kibana, which integrates seamlessly with Elasticsearch to provide a rich user interface for log analysis and monitoring.

bashCopy code

Command: kubectl port-forward svc/kibana 5601:5601

Furthermore, Fluentd offers flexibility and extensibility through its plugin ecosystem, allowing users to customize their log aggregation pipelines to suit their specific requirements. Users can install and configure Fluentd plugins to enrich log data, filter logs based on custom criteria, or forward logs to multiple destinations for redundancy or compliance purposes.

In addition to centralized log storage and analysis, Elasticsearch and Fluentd support features like log parsing, normalization, and alerting, enabling organizations to implement comprehensive log management solutions. By aggregating logs from various sources into a centralized repository, organizations can simplify troubleshooting, auditing, and compliance processes, ultimately improving the overall reliability and security of their distributed systems.

In summary, log aggregation strategies using tools like Elasticsearch and Fluentd play a crucial role in managing and monitoring distributed systems. By centralizing log data, organizations can gain visibility into system behavior, diagnose issues more effectively, and ensure the reliability and performance of their applications. With Elasticsearch providing powerful indexing and querying capabilities and Fluentd serving as a flexible log collector, organizations can build robust log aggregation pipelines to meet their logging and monitoring requirements in modern cloud-native environments.

Chapter 6: Real-Time Monitoring and Alerting Strategies for Microservices

Setting up real-time monitoring with Prometheus and Grafana is essential for effectively monitoring the health and performance of modern distributed systems. Prometheus is an open-source monitoring solution that collects metrics from various sources, while Grafana provides a powerful visualization platform for analyzing and presenting these metrics in real-time dashboards. Together, they form a powerful combination for monitoring and alerting in cloud-native environments.

bashCopy code

Command: kubectl apply -f prometheus.yaml

To set up Prometheus, Kubernetes users can deploy the Prometheus server as a StatefulSet using YAML manifests. These manifests define the configuration for the Prometheus server, including service discovery mechanisms, retention policies, and alerting rules. Prometheus supports multiple service discovery mechanisms, such as Kubernetes service discovery, DNS-based service discovery, and static configuration, allowing users to dynamically discover and monitor services running in their Kubernetes clusters.

yamlCopy code

prometheus.yaml apiVersion: v1 kind: ConfigMap metadata: name: prometheus-config data: prometheus.yml: | global: scrape_interval: 15s scrape_configs: - job_name: 'kubernetes-nodes'

```
kubernetes_sd_configs: - role: node - job_name:
'kubernetes-pods' kubernetes_sd_configs: - role: pod
```

Once Prometheus is deployed, it starts collecting metrics from various endpoints exposed by applications and infrastructure components. Kubernetes users can configure Prometheus to scrape metrics from Kubernetes nodes, pods, services, and other resources using Kubernetes service discovery. Prometheus supports multiple exporters, which are agents that expose metrics in a format that Prometheus can scrape. For example, the Node Exporter exposes system-level metrics from Kubernetes nodes, while the kube-state-metrics exporter exposes metrics about Kubernetes objects like pods, services, and deployments.

bashCopy code

Command: kubectl apply -f grafana.yaml

After setting up Prometheus, the next step is to deploy Grafana, which provides a user-friendly interface for creating dashboards and visualizing metrics collected by Prometheus. Kubernetes users can deploy Grafana using Helm charts, which simplify the deployment and configuration process. Helm charts allow users to specify configuration options such as data sources, dashboards, and plugins, making it easy to customize Grafana according to their monitoring requirements.

yamlCopy code

```
# grafana.yaml apiVersion: v1 kind: ConfigMap
metadata: name: grafana-config data: grafana.ini: |
datasources: - name: Prometheus type: prometheus
access: proxy orgId: 1 url: http://prometheus:9090
isDefault: true
```

Once Grafana is deployed, users can access the Grafana web interface using a web browser and configure data sources to connect to Prometheus. By adding Prometheus as a data source, users can query and visualize metrics collected by Prometheus in Grafana dashboards. Grafana supports various visualization options, including graphs, charts, tables, and heatmaps, allowing users to create custom dashboards tailored to their monitoring needs.

In addition to visualization, Grafana also supports alerting, allowing users to define alert rules based on metric thresholds or other conditions. Users can configure alert rules in Grafana and receive notifications via email, Slack, or other channels when an alert condition is triggered. This enables proactive monitoring and alerting, helping teams detect and respond to issues before they impact the availability or performance of their systems.

In summary, setting up real-time monitoring with Prometheus and Grafana is a critical aspect of managing and monitoring modern distributed systems. By deploying Prometheus to collect metrics and Grafana to visualize and analyze these metrics, organizations can gain valuable insights into the health and performance of their applications and infrastructure. With features like service discovery, exporters, data sources, and dashboards, Prometheus and Grafana provide a comprehensive monitoring solution for cloud-native environments, enabling teams to monitor, troubleshoot, and optimize their systems effectively.

Alerting in microservices environments is crucial for identifying and addressing issues promptly, ensuring the reliability and availability of services. Effective alerting practices help teams detect abnormal behavior, anomalies, and potential failures before they escalate into critical incidents. By establishing clear alerting strategies, configuring appropriate thresholds, and leveraging automation, organizations can minimize downtime, maintain service quality, and meet their service level objectives (SLOs).

To implement effective alerting in microservices environments, organizations should start by defining clear objectives and priorities for their alerting system. This involves identifying key metrics, service level indicators (SLIs), and thresholds that indicate normal operation and potential issues. Teams should establish guidelines for severity levels, escalation policies, and response times based on the impact and urgency of alerts.

bashCopy code

```
Command: kubectl apply -f prometheus-alertmanager.yaml
```

One of the essential components of an alerting system is the alert manager, which is responsible for processing alerts generated by monitoring systems and taking appropriate actions. In Kubernetes environments, the Alertmanager component can be deployed as part of the Prometheus monitoring stack. The Alertmanager receives alerts from Prometheus, applies deduplication, aggregation, and routing rules, and forwards alerts to notification channels such as email, Slack, or PagerDuty.

yamlCopy code

```
# prometheus-alertmanager.yaml apiVersion: v1 kind: ConfigMap metadata: name: alertmanager-config data: alertmanager.yml: | global: resolve_timeout: 5m route: group_by: ['alertname', 'cluster', 'service'] group_wait: 10s group_interval: 10m repeat_interval: 1h receiver: 'slack-notifications' receivers: - name: 'slack-notifications' slack_configs: - api_url: 'https://hooks.slack.com/services/XXXXXXXXX/YYYYYYYYY/ZZZZZZZZZZZZZZZZZZZZZZZZ' channel: '#alerts' send_resolved: true
```

Once the alert manager is configured, teams should define alerting rules based on their monitoring requirements and business priorities. Alerting rules specify conditions that trigger alerts when certain thresholds are breached or specific conditions are met. These rules can be defined using PromQL (Prometheus Query Language) expressions to query metrics collected by Prometheus and generate alerts based on predefined criteria.

yamlCopy code

```
# prometheus-rules.yaml apiVersion: monitoring.coreos.com/v1 kind: PrometheusRule metadata: name: alerting-rules spec: groups: - name: example rules: - alert: HighErrorRate expr: sum(rate(http_requests_total{status="500"}[5m])) / sum(rate(http_requests_total[5m])) > 0.05 for: 10m labels: severity: critical annotations: description:
```

'High error rate detected on {{ $labels.service }}.'
summary: 'High error rate on {{ $labels.service }}.'
In addition to defining alerting rules, teams should establish robust notification channels and escalation policies to ensure that alerts are communicated to the appropriate stakeholders promptly. Notifications can be sent to communication platforms such as Slack, Microsoft Teams, or email, allowing teams to collaborate and coordinate their response efforts effectively. Moreover, automated escalation policies can ensure that critical alerts are escalated to on-call engineers or incident response teams if they are not acknowledged or resolved within a specified timeframe.

bashCopy code

Command: kubectl apply -f prometheus-rules.yaml

Regular testing and validation of alerting rules are essential to ensure their effectiveness and reliability. Teams should conduct tabletop exercises, simulations, and game days to test their alerting system's response to different scenarios and verify that alerts are triggered appropriately. Additionally, teams should continuously monitor and review their alerting system's performance, fine-tuning alerting rules, thresholds, and notification channels based on feedback and real-world incidents.

In summary, implementing effective alerting practices is essential for maintaining the reliability, availability, and performance of microservices environments. By defining clear objectives, configuring appropriate alerting rules, and establishing robust notification channels and escalation policies, organizations can detect and respond to issues promptly, minimizing downtime and ensuring a seamless user experience. With proactive monitoring, automation, and regular testing, teams can build a resilient alerting system that helps them stay ahead of potential disruptions and meet their service level objectives.

Chapter 7: Performance Optimization and Capacity Planning in Microservices Environments

Performance profiling is a critical aspect of optimizing microservices architecture, ensuring that applications meet desired performance benchmarks and deliver a responsive user experience. It involves analyzing various aspects of system behavior, identifying bottlenecks, and optimizing resource utilization to enhance overall performance. Performance profiling techniques provide insights into application performance characteristics, enabling developers to diagnose and address performance issues effectively.

One commonly used technique for performance profiling is **CPU Profiling**, which involves measuring the amount of CPU time consumed by different parts of an application. CPU profiling helps identify CPU-intensive tasks and areas of code that may be causing performance bottlenecks. In Go programming language, for example, developers can use the built-in pprof tool to generate CPU profiles and analyze CPU usage. The following command can be used to enable CPU profiling for a Go application:

bashCopy code

```
go                    tool                    pprof
http://localhost:6060/debug/pprof/profile
```

This command starts a CPU profile server for the specified Go application, allowing developers to capture CPU profiles and analyze them using tools like pprof.

Once the profiling data is collected, developers can analyze it to identify hotspots and optimize performance-critical code paths.

Another essential technique for performance profiling is **Memory Profiling**, which involves measuring the memory consumption and allocation patterns of an application. Memory profiling helps identify memory leaks, excessive memory usage, and inefficient memory allocation patterns that can impact application performance. In Go, developers can use the pprof tool to generate memory profiles and analyze memory usage. The following command can be used to enable memory profiling for a Go application:

bashCopy code

```
go tool pprof http://localhost:6060/debug/pprof/heap
```

This command starts a memory profile server for the specified Go application, allowing developers to capture memory profiles and analyze them using pprof. Memory profiling data provides insights into memory allocation patterns, object lifetimes, and memory consumption, helping developers optimize memory usage and prevent memory-related performance issues.

In addition to CPU and memory profiling, **Network Profiling** is another important technique for analyzing the performance of microservices architecture. Network profiling involves measuring network latency, throughput, and error rates to identify network-related performance bottlenecks and optimize network communication. Tools like Wireshark, tcpdump, and Netdata can be used to capture and analyze network traffic, providing insights into network behavior and performance characteristics. By analyzing network profiling data, developers can identify inefficient network protocols, excessive network round-trips, and other network-related issues that may impact application performance.

Database Profiling is another essential technique for optimizing the performance of microservices architecture, especially in systems that rely heavily on database operations. Database profiling involves measuring database query performance, indexing strategies, and database server resource utilization to identify database-related performance bottlenecks and optimize database performance. Developers can use database profiling tools like MySQL Performance Schema, pg_stat_statements in PostgreSQL, or SQL Server Profiler in Microsoft SQL Server to capture and analyze database performance metrics. By analyzing database profiling data, developers can identify slow-performing queries, inefficient indexing strategies, and other database-related issues that may impact application performance.

Application Profiling is a comprehensive technique that combines CPU, memory, network, and database profiling to analyze the overall performance of microservices architecture. By profiling various aspects of the application stack, including code execution, memory usage, network communication, and database operations, developers can gain a holistic view of application performance and identify performance bottlenecks across different layers of the system. Application profiling helps developers optimize performance-critical components, improve resource utilization, and enhance overall application performance.

In summary, performance profiling techniques play a crucial role in optimizing the performance of microservices architecture, ensuring that applications meet desired performance benchmarks and deliver a responsive user experience. By employing CPU profiling, memory profiling, network profiling, database profiling, and application profiling, developers can gain insights into application performance characteristics, identify performance bottlenecks, and optimize resource utilization to enhance overall performance. With effective performance profiling, developers can build high-performance microservices applications that meet the demands of modern distributed systems.

Capacity planning is a critical aspect of managing microservices architecture, especially when dealing with traffic spikes that can significantly impact application performance and availability. Effective capacity planning strategies enable organizations to anticipate and prepare for increased demand, ensuring that their systems can handle sudden surges in traffic without experiencing downtime or performance degradation. By carefully analyzing workload patterns, resource utilization, and performance metrics, organizations can determine the optimal infrastructure configuration and scaling policies to accommodate traffic spikes efficiently.

One essential capacity planning strategy is **Performance Monitoring and Analysis**, which involves continuously monitoring key performance metrics such as CPU utilization, memory usage, disk I/O, and network throughput. Tools like Prometheus, Grafana, and Datadog provide comprehensive monitoring capabilities, allowing organizations to track system performance in real-time and identify performance bottlenecks proactively. By analyzing performance metrics over time, organizations can gain insights into workload patterns and resource utilization trends, enabling them to make informed decisions about infrastructure provisioning and scaling.

Horizontal Scaling is another important capacity planning strategy that involves adding more instances of microservices to distribute the workload across multiple servers. Cloud platforms like Amazon Web Services (AWS), Google Cloud Platform (GCP), and Microsoft Azure provide auto-scaling features that automatically adjust the number of instances based on workload demand. For example, organizations can use AWS Auto Scaling to automatically add or remove EC2 instances based on predefined scaling policies. The following AWS CLI command can be used to create an auto-scaling group:

```bash
aws autoscaling create-auto-scaling-group --auto-scaling-group-name my-asg --launch-configuration-name my-lc --min-size 2 --max-size 10 --desired-capacity 2
```

This command creates an auto-scaling group named "my-asg" with a minimum size of 2 instances, a maximum size of 10 instances, and a desired capacity of 2 instances. By leveraging horizontal scaling, organizations can dynamically adjust their infrastructure capacity to handle traffic spikes effectively while minimizing costs and maximizing resource utilization.

Vertical Scaling is another capacity planning strategy that involves increasing the computational resources (e.g., CPU, memory) of individual servers to handle increased workload demand. While vertical scaling can be effective for scaling up individual microservices instances, it may have limitations in terms of scalability and cost-efficiency compared to horizontal scaling. However, organizations can use vertical scaling in conjunction with horizontal scaling to optimize performance and resource utilization. For example, organizations can use Kubernetes Horizontal Pod Autoscaler (HPA) to automatically adjust the number of pods based on CPU utilization. The following command can be used to enable HPA for a Kubernetes deployment:

bashCopy code

```
kubectl autoscale deployment my-deployment --cpu-percent=50 --min=1 --max=10
```

This command creates an HPA object for the "my-deployment" deployment, specifying that the number of pods should scale based on CPU utilization, with a target CPU utilization of 50%, a minimum of 1 pod, and a maximum of 10 pods. By leveraging vertical scaling, organizations can optimize the performance of individual microservices instances and handle traffic spikes more efficiently.

Load Testing is a critical aspect of capacity planning that involves simulating various traffic scenarios to assess the performance and scalability of microservices architecture under different load conditions. Tools like Apache JMeter, Gatling, and Locust can be used to simulate thousands or millions of concurrent users accessing the application simultaneously. By conducting load tests, organizations can identify performance bottlenecks, validate scaling policies, and determine the maximum capacity of their systems. Load testing also helps organizations validate their disaster recovery plans and ensure that their systems can handle unexpected traffic spikes without experiencing downtime or performance degradation.

Fault Injection is another capacity planning strategy that involves deliberately introducing failures into the system to assess its resilience and ability to handle adverse conditions. By injecting faults such as network latency, packet loss, and service unavailability, organizations can evaluate the impact of failures on application performance and identify areas for improvement. Tools like Chaos Monkey, Gremlin, and Netflix Simian Army provide capabilities for conducting fault injection experiments in production environments safely. By proactively identifying and addressing weaknesses in their systems, organizations can enhance their resilience and ensure that their microservices architecture can handle traffic spikes and other operational challenges effectively.

In summary, capacity planning is a crucial aspect of managing microservices architecture and ensuring that systems can handle traffic spikes and other workload fluctuations effectively. By employing performance monitoring and analysis, horizontal and vertical scaling, load testing, and fault injection, organizations can optimize their infrastructure configuration, scalability policies, and resilience mechanisms to meet the demands of modern distributed systems. With effective capacity planning strategies in place, organizations can minimize the risk of downtime, maximize resource utilization, and deliver a reliable and responsive user experience.

Chapter 8: Proactive Maintenance Techniques for Microservices: Health Checks and Self-Healing Systems

Implementing health checks for microservices is a crucial aspect of maintaining system reliability and ensuring seamless operation in distributed environments. Health checks provide real-time insights into the status and availability of microservices, allowing organizations to detect and address issues proactively before they escalate into larger problems. By continuously monitoring the health of individual microservices and their dependencies, organizations can minimize downtime, improve fault tolerance, and deliver a more resilient user experience.

One common approach to implementing health checks is by **defining a Health Endpoint** for each microservice. A health endpoint is a URL exposed by the microservice that provides information about its current health status. Typically, this endpoint returns a simple response indicating whether the microservice is healthy or experiencing issues. For example, in a Node.js application, you can create a health endpoint using Express.js:

javascriptCopy code

```
const express = require('express'); const app = express(); app.get('/health', (req, res) => { // Perform health checks here const isHealthy = true; if (isHealthy) { res.status(200).json({ status: 'healthy' });
```

```
} else { res.status(500).json({ status: 'unhealthy' }); }
}); app.listen(3000, () => { console.log('Server is
running on port 3000'); });
```

In this example, the **/health** endpoint returns a JSON
response with a status of 'healthy' if the microservice is
operating normally. If any issues are detected during
the health check, the endpoint returns a status of
'unhealthy' along with an appropriate HTTP status code.

Container Orchestration Platforms like Kubernetes
provide built-in support for health checks, allowing
organizations to define health probes for their
microservices. Kubernetes supports three types of
health checks: livenessProbe, readinessProbe, and
startupProbe. These probes enable Kubernetes to
monitor the health of microservices and automatically
restart or remove unhealthy instances. Below is an
example of defining health probes in a Kubernetes
Deployment YAML file:

yamlCopy code

```
apiVersion: apps/v1 kind: Deployment metadata:
name: my-deployment spec: replicas: 3 selector:
matchLabels: app: my-app template: metadata:
labels: app: my-app spec: containers: - name: my-
container image: my-image:latest readinessProbe:
httpGet: path: /health port: 8080
initialDelaySeconds: 5 periodSeconds: 10
livenessProbe: httpGet: path: /health port: 8080
initialDelaySeconds: 10 periodSeconds: 20
```

In this YAML configuration, the **readinessProbe** and
livenessProbe sections define HTTP health checks that

Kubernetes will perform on the **/health** endpoint of each pod. Kubernetes will periodically send HTTP requests to the health endpoint to determine whether the microservice is ready to accept traffic (**readinessProbe**) or whether it needs to be restarted (**livenessProbe**).

Another approach to implementing health checks is by **leveraging External Monitoring Tools**. External monitoring tools like Prometheus, Grafana, and Datadog can be used to collect and analyze health metrics from microservices. These tools provide customizable dashboards, alerting mechanisms, and historical data analysis capabilities, allowing organizations to gain deeper insights into the health of their microservices. By integrating external monitoring tools with microservices architecture, organizations can centralize health monitoring, streamline troubleshooting, and ensure proactive incident response.

Furthermore, **Database Health Checks** are essential for ensuring the overall health of microservices that rely on databases. Database health checks involve monitoring database performance metrics such as connection pool usage, query execution times, and database server resource utilization. Tools like New Relic, Dynatrace, and AppDynamics offer database monitoring capabilities that enable organizations to detect database-related issues early and optimize database performance for microservices applications.

Additionally, **Continuous Integration/Continuous Deployment (CI/CD) Pipelines** play a crucial role in automating the deployment of microservices and conducting health checks as part of the deployment process. CI/CD pipelines can include automated tests and health checks to verify the integrity of microservices before they are deployed to production environments. By integrating health checks into CI/CD pipelines, organizations can ensure that only healthy microservices are deployed, reducing the risk of introducing issues into production environments.

In summary, implementing health checks for microservices is essential for maintaining system reliability, minimizing downtime, and delivering a seamless user experience. By defining health endpoints, leveraging container orchestration platforms, utilizing external monitoring tools, conducting database health checks, and integrating health checks into CI/CD pipelines, organizations can effectively monitor the health of their microservices, detect issues proactively, and ensure the overall health and stability of their distributed systems.

Self-healing systems represent a crucial aspect of modern microservices architecture, providing automated remediation capabilities to address failures and maintain system reliability without human intervention. These systems leverage advanced monitoring, alerting, and orchestration mechanisms to detect anomalies and apply corrective actions in real-time, thereby minimizing downtime and ensuring uninterrupted service delivery.

One key component of self-healing systems is **Automated Remediation**, which involves automatically resolving issues detected by monitoring systems without human intervention. Automated remediation relies on predefined remediation playbooks or scripts that outline the steps to be taken in response to specific events or conditions. These playbooks can include actions such as restarting failed services, scaling up or down resources, or rerouting traffic to healthy instances.

For instance, in a Kubernetes cluster, organizations can define **Horizontal Pod Autoscalers (HPA)** to automatically adjust the number of running instances based on CPU or memory utilization metrics. This can be achieved using the following command:

```
bashCopy code
kubectl autoscale deployment <deployment-name> --cpu-percent=70 --min=2 --max=10
```

In this command, the **--cpu-percent** flag specifies the target CPU utilization percentage, while **--min** and **--max** define the minimum and maximum number of instances to maintain.

Moreover, self-healing systems often leverage **Health Checks** to continuously monitor the status and health of microservices. These health checks can be configured to periodically probe microservices endpoints and validate their responsiveness. If a microservice fails to respond or returns an error, the monitoring system triggers automated remediation actions to address the issue.

Another crucial aspect of self-healing systems is **Fault Tolerance**. By designing microservices applications with fault tolerance in mind, organizations can minimize the impact of failures and disruptions. This involves implementing redundancy, failover mechanisms, and circuit breakers to ensure that failures in one component do not cascade to other parts of the system. In addition to reactive measures, self-healing systems also employ **Predictive Analytics** to anticipate and prevent potential issues before they occur. By analyzing historical data and trends, these systems can identify patterns indicative of impending failures and take proactive measures to mitigate risks. For example, machine learning algorithms can analyze application performance metrics and predict when certain components are likely to fail based on past behavior.

Furthermore, **Automated Incident Response** is a critical aspect of self-healing systems, enabling organizations to respond rapidly to incidents and minimize the impact on users. Automated incident response workflows can include actions such as notifying stakeholders, rolling back deployments, or triggering automated tests to validate fixes. These workflows are typically orchestrated using tools like Jenkins, GitLab CI/CD, or Ansible Tower.

Moreover, self-healing systems can leverage **Infrastructure as Code (IaC)** principles to automate the provisioning and configuration of infrastructure resources. By defining infrastructure resources in code using tools like Terraform or AWS CloudFormation, organizations can easily recreate and redeploy infrastructure in case of failures or outages.

Additionally, **Chaos Engineering** practices play a vital role in validating the resilience of self-healing systems. Chaos engineering involves deliberately injecting failures and faults into the system to test its resilience and observe how it responds. By conducting chaos experiments in controlled environments, organizations can identify weaknesses and areas for improvement in their self-healing capabilities.

In summary, self-healing systems are essential for maintaining the reliability and resilience of microservices architectures. By automating remediation, leveraging health checks, ensuring fault tolerance, employing predictive analytics, automating incident response, leveraging infrastructure as code, and practicing chaos engineering, organizations can build robust self-healing systems that can detect, respond to, and recover from failures autonomously, ensuring uninterrupted service delivery and a seamless user experience.

Chapter 9: Microservices Versioning and Dependency Management

Versioning strategies for microservices APIs are crucial for managing changes and ensuring compatibility between different versions of services. Effective versioning allows developers to introduce new features, fix bugs, and evolve APIs while minimizing disruption to existing clients. There are several approaches to versioning microservices APIs, each with its benefits and trade-offs.

One commonly used approach is **URI Versioning**, where the API version is included directly in the URI path. This approach makes it explicit which version of the API the client is accessing and allows for easy differentiation between different versions. For example, a URI versioning approach might look like this:

bashCopy code

GET /api/v1/resource

In this example, **/api/v1/** indicates that the client is accessing version 1 of the API. Subsequent versions would have their version numbers incremented accordingly, such as **/api/v2/**, **/api/v3/**, and so on.

Another approach is **Query Parameter Versioning**, where the version information is included as a query parameter in the URL. For example:

bashCopy code

GET /api/resource?version=1

While this approach keeps the URI cleaner compared to URI versioning, it may lead to caching issues and can make it harder to manage different versions of the API over time.

A third approach is **Header Versioning**, where the version information is included as a custom header in the HTTP request. This approach keeps the URI clean and allows for more flexibility in versioning. For example:

bashCopy code

GET /api/resource X-API-Version: 1

Header versioning can be particularly useful when dealing with complex APIs or when the versioning information needs to be hidden from the client.

Additionally, **Content Negotiation** can be used to negotiate the API version based on the **Accept** header in the HTTP request. This approach allows clients to specify their preferred version of the API and enables the server to return the appropriate representation. For example:

bashCopy code

GET /api/resource Accept: application/vnd.company.resource.v1+json

In this example, the client specifies that it prefers version 1 of the API in JSON format.

Furthermore, **Semantic Versioning** (SemVer) is often used to version APIs, especially when following a URI versioning scheme. Semantic Versioning consists of three parts: MAJOR.MINOR.PATCH. A change in the MAJOR version indicates backward-incompatible changes, a change in the MINOR version indicates backward-compatible feature additions, and a change in the PATCH version indicates backward-compatible bug fixes.

For example, if a breaking change is introduced, the MAJOR version would be incremented:

bashCopy code

GET /api/v2/resource

Similarly, if a new feature is added in a backward-compatible manner, the MINOR version would be incremented:

bashCopy code

GET /api/v1.1/resource

And if a bug fix is made without changing the API contract, the PATCH version would be incremented:

bashCopy code

GET /api/v1.0.1/resource

Implementing versioning strategies often involves careful planning and consideration of backward compatibility, deprecation policies, and communication with API consumers. It's essential to document versioning policies and provide clear guidance to clients on how to migrate to newer versions when necessary.

Moreover, when deploying microservices with different versions of APIs, it's crucial to ensure proper testing and validation to prevent unintended consequences or regressions. Continuous integration and continuous deployment (CI/CD) pipelines can automate the testing and deployment of new versions, helping to streamline the release process and reduce the risk of errors.

In summary, versioning strategies for microservices APIs play a critical role in managing change, ensuring compatibility, and facilitating the evolution of software systems over time. By choosing the right versioning approach, following semantic versioning principles, implementing content negotiation, and leveraging CI/CD pipelines, organizations can effectively manage API versions and provide a seamless experience for API consumers.

Dependency management is a critical aspect of software development, ensuring that projects can efficiently manage and utilize external libraries, frameworks, and modules. With the proliferation of open-source software and the increasing complexity of modern applications, effective dependency management tools and techniques are essential for maintaining project stability, security, and scalability. Among the various tools available for dependency management, Git and dependency injection are two widely used approaches that offer distinct benefits and functionalities.

Git, a distributed version control system, is a fundamental tool for managing source code and its dependencies. It provides developers with the ability to track changes, collaborate with team members, and integrate external libraries seamlessly into their projects. One of Git's key features is its submodule functionality, which allows developers to include external repositories as subdirectories within their own repositories. This enables projects to depend on specific versions of external libraries or frameworks while maintaining a clear separation of concerns.

To add a submodule to a Git repository, developers can use the following command:

bashCopy code

```
git submodule add <repository_url> <directory>
```

For example, to add the "example_library" repository as a submodule in the "libs" directory, the command would be:

bashCopy code

```
git                    submodule                    add
```
https://github.com/example/example_library
libs/example_library

Once added, the submodule can be initialized and updated with the following commands:

bashCopy code

git submodule init git submodule update

This ensures that the submodule is cloned and synchronized with the appropriate version specified in the parent repository.

While Git provides a mechanism for managing external dependencies, dependency injection is a design pattern commonly used in object-oriented programming to manage the dependencies of components within a system. Dependency injection promotes loose coupling between components by allowing dependencies to be passed to a class from an external source rather than being instantiated internally. This makes classes more modular, testable, and reusable, as they are not tightly coupled to specific implementations of their dependencies.

In languages like Java, Spring Framework provides robust support for dependency injection through its Inversion of Control (IoC) container. With Spring IoC, developers can declare dependencies using annotations or XML configuration files and let the container manage the instantiation and injection of dependencies at runtime. This decouples the components from their dependencies and allows for easy configuration and swapping of implementations.

To illustrate dependency injection in Spring, consider the following example:

```
javaCopy code
public class UserService { private final UserRepository
userRepository;              @Autowired              public
UserService(UserRepository       userRepository)      {
this.userRepository = userRepository; } // Other methods
using userRepository }
```

In this example, the **UserService** class declares a dependency on the **UserRepository** interface. By annotating the constructor with **@Autowired**, Spring will automatically inject an instance of the **UserRepository** interface when creating a **UserService** bean.

In addition to Spring, other dependency injection frameworks and libraries are available for different programming languages and platforms, each offering similar capabilities for managing dependencies in applications.

Overall, effective dependency management is crucial for the success of software projects, and tools like Git and dependency injection play significant roles in achieving this goal. By leveraging Git submodules to manage external dependencies and adopting dependency injection to manage internal dependencies, developers can build modular, maintainable, and scalable applications that meet the evolving needs of users and stakeholders.

Chapter 10: Post-Mortem Analysis and Continuous Improvement Practices for Microservices Systems

Post-incident reviews, also known as postmortems or blameless retrospectives, are essential processes for organizations utilizing microservices architectures to ensure continuous improvement and resilience in their systems. When a microservice outage occurs, conducting a thorough post-incident review is crucial for identifying the root causes of the incident, learning from the experience, and implementing preventive measures to minimize the risk of similar outages in the future.

To initiate a post-incident review, the first step is to gather all relevant information about the incident, including timelines, affected services, and any actions taken during the incident response. This information can be collected from incident management tools, monitoring systems, and communication channels used by the incident response team.

Once the incident data is collected, the next step is to convene a post-incident review meeting with key stakeholders, including engineers, developers, operations teams, and business representatives. The goal of the meeting is to analyze the incident in detail, discuss its impact on users and the business, and identify contributing factors and potential areas for improvement.

During the post-incident review meeting, it is essential to maintain a blameless environment where team members feel comfortable sharing their observations and insights without fear of reprisal. This encourages open communication and collaboration, enabling the team to focus on identifying systemic issues rather than assigning blame to individuals.

One effective technique for conducting post-incident reviews is the "Five Whys" method, which involves asking "why" repeatedly to drill down to the root cause of the incident. By iteratively probing deeper into the causes of the incident, the team can uncover underlying issues that may have contributed to the outage.

For example, if the incident was caused by a database failure, asking "why did the database fail?" may lead to insights such as inadequate capacity planning or lack of automated failover mechanisms. By asking "why" multiple times, the team can uncover systemic issues that need to be addressed to prevent similar incidents in the future.

In addition to the Five Whys method, other techniques such as fault tree analysis, timeline analysis, and postmortem templates can also be valuable tools for conducting post-incident reviews. These techniques help structure the review process, facilitate data analysis, and ensure that all relevant aspects of the incident are thoroughly examined.

Once the root causes of the incident have been identified, the next step is to develop action items or remediation plans to address the underlying issues. These action items may include implementing technical improvements, updating documentation, enhancing monitoring and alerting systems, or revising operational procedures.

It is essential to prioritize action items based on their potential impact on system reliability and user experience. High-priority items that address critical vulnerabilities or systemic issues should be addressed promptly, while lower-priority items can be scheduled for future iterations or releases.

After the post-incident review meeting, it is crucial to document the findings, action items, and follow-up tasks in a postmortem report or incident analysis document. This document serves as a reference for the incident response team and other stakeholders and provides valuable insights for future incident prevention and mitigation efforts.

In addition to addressing technical aspects of the incident, post-incident reviews should also consider organizational and cultural factors that may have contributed to the outage. This includes evaluating communication protocols, decision-making processes, and team dynamics to identify opportunities for improvement.

Continuous learning and improvement are central to the success of microservices architectures, and post-incident reviews play a vital role in this process. By conducting thorough reviews of incidents, identifying root causes, and implementing corrective actions, organizations can enhance the resilience, reliability, and performance of their microservices systems over time.

Establishing a culture of continuous improvement in microservices development is essential for organizations striving to adapt to the dynamic nature of modern software development. This culture emphasizes iterative learning, experimentation, and feedback loops to drive ongoing enhancements to products and processes. A key aspect of fostering this culture is promoting transparency and collaboration among development teams, encouraging them to share knowledge, insights, and best practices. One way to facilitate collaboration is through the use of version control systems like Git, which allow developers to work concurrently on codebases, track changes, and review each other's code using pull requests. By leveraging Git workflows such as feature branching and code reviews, teams can ensure that changes are thoroughly vetted and aligned with project goals before being merged into the main codebase.

Furthermore, embracing agile methodologies such as Scrum or Kanban can help teams organize their work into manageable iterations or flow-based processes, enabling them to deliver value to customers more frequently and adapt to changing requirements more effectively. Agile practices emphasize close collaboration between cross-functional teams, regular sprint planning, and retrospective meetings to reflect on past performance and identify areas for improvement. For example, using the Agile methodology, teams can break down complex features into smaller, more manageable tasks, prioritize work based on customer feedback and business value, and deliver working software incrementally, allowing for rapid iteration and validation of ideas.

Continuous integration (CI) and continuous delivery (CD) pipelines are indispensable tools for automating the software development lifecycle and enabling teams to release changes quickly and safely. CI/CD pipelines automate the process of building, testing, and deploying software, allowing teams to detect and fix defects early in the development process and deliver features to customers faster. Tools like Jenkins, CircleCI, and GitLab CI/CD enable developers to define CI/CD pipelines as code, version control them alongside application code, and execute them automatically whenever changes are made to the codebase. By integrating automated tests, code quality checks, and deployment scripts into CI/CD pipelines, teams can ensure that changes are thoroughly validated and safely deployed to production environments with minimal manual intervention.

Implementing infrastructure as code (IaC) practices is another essential aspect of establishing a culture of continuous improvement in microservices development. IaC enables teams to manage infrastructure configurations programmatically using code, allowing for versioning, code review, and automation of infrastructure provisioning and management tasks. Tools like Terraform, AWS CloudFormation, and Azure Resource Manager provide declarative syntax for defining infrastructure resources and dependencies, enabling teams to create reproducible and scalable environments across development, staging, and production environments. By treating infrastructure as code, teams can leverage the same development practices used for application code, such as version control, automated testing, and continuous integration, to ensure that infrastructure changes are reliable, consistent, and well-documented.

In addition to technical practices, fostering a culture of continuous improvement requires a supportive organizational environment that encourages learning, experimentation, and risk-taking. This includes providing opportunities for professional development, promoting knowledge sharing and collaboration, and recognizing and rewarding innovation and initiative. For example, organizations can establish guilds or communities of practice where developers can exchange ideas, share experiences, and learn from each other's successes and failures. By fostering a culture of psychological safety and empowerment, organizations can encourage employees to take ownership of their work, experiment with new technologies and approaches, and contribute to the overall success of the organization.

Furthermore, embracing DevOps principles can help organizations break down silos between development and operations teams, enabling them to work together more effectively to deliver value to customers. DevOps emphasizes collaboration, automation, and measurement, enabling teams to streamline the software delivery process, reduce lead times, and improve the reliability and quality of software deployments. By adopting DevOps practices such as infrastructure as code, continuous integration and delivery, automated testing, and monitoring and observability, organizations can accelerate the pace of innovation, increase the resilience of their systems, and deliver better outcomes for customers.

Ultimately, establishing a culture of continuous improvement in microservices development requires a holistic approach that addresses technical, organizational, and cultural factors. By embracing agile methodologies, CI/CD practices, infrastructure as code, DevOps principles, and fostering a supportive and collaborative work environment, organizations can empower their teams to innovate, adapt to change, and deliver value to customers more effectively and efficiently.

Conclusion

In summary, "Microservices: Novice to Ninja - Build, Design, and Deploy Distributed Services" is a comprehensive book bundle that equips readers with the knowledge and skills needed to navigate the complex world of microservices architecture. Across four insightful volumes, this bundle provides a step-by-step journey from understanding the fundamentals of distributed systems to mastering advanced techniques for optimizing performance and security.

In "Microservices 101: A Beginner's Guide to Understanding Distributed Systems," readers are introduced to the foundational concepts of microservices architecture, including the benefits of decoupling, scalability, and fault tolerance. This book lays the groundwork for understanding the challenges and opportunities inherent in distributed systems.

"Architecting Microservices: Strategies for Designing Scalable and Resilient Systems" builds upon this foundation by exploring strategies for designing microservices that are both scalable and resilient. Readers learn how to leverage design patterns, such as bounded contexts, aggregates, and event sourcing, to create systems that can adapt and evolve over time.

"Mastering Microservices: Advanced Techniques for Optimizing Performance and Security" delves into advanced topics such as performance optimization and security best practices. Readers gain insights into techniques for improving the performance of microservices, as well as strategies for securing sensitive data and mitigating common security threats.

Finally, "Microservices Mastery: Expert Insights into Deployment, Monitoring, and Maintenance" provides expert guidance on deploying, monitoring, and maintaining microservices in production environments. Readers learn how to leverage tools and techniques for automating deployment pipelines, monitoring system health, and troubleshooting issues in distributed systems.

Together, these four volumes offer a comprehensive roadmap for anyone looking to build, design, and deploy microservices at scale. Whether you're a novice exploring the world of distributed systems for the first time or a seasoned professional seeking to optimize the performance and security of your microservices architecture, "Microservices: Novice to Ninja" has something to offer for every level of expertise.